REIMAGINE THE EDUCATION SYSTEM IN AI WORLD

EMPOWERING LEARNERS TO
OUT-THINK THE MACHINE

DR. CHITRA JOSHI

This is a work of non-fiction. The events and the incidents mentioned in the book are true and real. However, some names and characteristics have been changed, some events have been compressed, and some dialogues have been recreated.

First Edition: May 2026
Printed in India

Printed at: Gapmeta Ventures Pvt. Ltd., Navi Mumbai
Typeset in Times New Roman

ISBN: 978-93-6070-946-4

Cover Design: Priya Vora

STORYMIRROR
Stories that reflect you

Publisher:	StoryMirror Infotech Pvt. Ltd. Unit No-F/705, 7th Floor, Kailas Corporate Lounge, Veer Savarkar Road, Vikhroli Park Site, Vikhroli West, Mumbai-400079, Maharashtra, India.
Web:	storymirror.com
Facebook:	@storymirror
Twitter:	@story_mirror
Instagram:	@storymirror
Email:	marketing@storymirror.com

DEDICATION

To the educators, leaders, and students who dare to imagine a better future, and to the children of India, whose potential inspires every innovation in learning.

TABLE OF CONTENTS

PREFACE

We live in a period where change is unprecedented. Artificial Intelligence (AI) is not just a technological milestone; it represents a fundamental shift in how we process information, solve problems, and connect with others. For those in the education sector, this shift raises a profound question: In a world where machines can think, what does it mean to be a learner?

This book is the bridge between our traditional classroom practices and the demands of an AI-driven future. While many focus on the disruption caused by AI, this book focuses on the transformation. It is guided by the framework of the National Education Policy (NEP) 2020, which speaks about the shift from rote learning to holistic, integrated, and learner-centred education.

The goal of this book is to move beyond the fear of the machine. It is designed for school leaders, teachers, and policymakers.

Each chapter includes strategic frameworks, case studies and reflection prompts.

We are preparing students not only for the workplace but also for a life of purpose. This book is a companion on that journey, helping you reimagine the classroom as a space where human potential is amplified, not replaced.

INTRODUCTION

For decades, the definition of a successful education was the accumulation of knowledge. Those who could remember the most, calculate the fastest, and reproduce facts most accurately were considered successful. Today, that has collapsed. We have entered an era where a child with a smartphone has more "knowledge" on his/her fingertips than the greatest scholars of the last century combined.

As Artificial Intelligence (AI) becomes a part of our lives, we are forced to confront a radical question: If AI knows more than us, what is the classroom for?

1. The Purpose of Education in an Automated World

In an AI-driven world, the purpose of education shifts from content mastery to context mastery. It is no longer enough to know the "what," students must understand the "why" and the "how."

Education must now serve as the forge for human identity. It is about developing the wisdom to use powerful tools ethically, the curiosity to ask the right questions, and the strength to navigate a world where the only constant is change. Guided by NEP 2020, we must view education not as a preparation for a specific job, but as the development of a "whole human" capable of thriving alongside intelligent machines.

2. The New Non-Negotiables: Human-Centric Skills

When technical tasks and data processing are automated, "soft skills" become the "hard skills" of the future. We must change the course of our curriculum toward three non-negotiable pillars:

- Critical Inquiry & Metacognition: Learning how to think about thinking. In a world of AI-generated content, the ability to discern truth from hallucination is a survival skill.
- Empathy and Social AI: The ability to connect, lead, and collaborate. These are the uniquely human traits that AI cannot authentically replicate.
- Adaptive Creativity: Using AI as a co-pilot to solve complex, real-world problems that don't have a textbook answer.

3. Beyond the Exam: Redefining Measurement

Perhaps the greatest challenge we face is our obsession with the high-stakes exam. If an AI can pass a standardized test better than a human, then the test is no longer measuring human potential; it is measuring machine-like retrieval.

To truly measure learning in this new era, we must move away from the "center-stage exam" and toward:

- Process-Based Assessment: Evaluating how a student arrived at a solution, not just the final answer.
- Continuous Feedback Loops: Using AI to provide real-time, personalized insights into a student's

growth, rather than a single grade at the end of the year.

- Portfolio & Project Evidence: Measuring competency through real-world applications and creative contributions.

The Path Ahead

We must move beyond competing with AI and begin to out think it. By aligning the wisdom of our pedagogical heritage with the power of modern technology, we can create an education system that is more human, not less.

CHAPTER 1

THE SYSTEM IS OUTDATED

Why is education breaking

We are trying to run 21st-century software on 19th-century hardware.

The primary problem with education is not the curriculum, teachers, or technology; rather, it lies in the design of the system itself. Most schools are not designed to produce thinkers; they are designed to produce workers who no longer exist in this world.

The Factory Model of Education — Why It Was Built This Way

Modern education did not begin as a broken system. It began as a solution.

The schooling structure most of us grew up in included fixed classrooms, age-based grades, standardized curricula, and uniform examinations, which were designed during a time of massive social and economic transition. Industrialization demanded a workforce that could follow instructions, arrive on time, perform repetitive tasks with consistency, and respect authority. Education, therefore, was shaped to meet the needs of factories, offices, and bureaucratic systems.

Uniformity was not a flaw then; it was a feature.

Teaching large groups the same content in the same way ensured scale. Standardized textbooks ensured consistency. Exams ensured comparability. Grades and ranks created clear filters for employment and higher education. In societies trying to move millions out of poverty, this system created order, predictability, and upward mobility.

For decades, it worked remarkably well.

The factory model produced engineers, doctors, administrators, accountants, and teachers who built institutions, infrastructure, and governance systems. It offered a shared baseline of literacy and numeracy across populations. In countries like India, it became a ladder, however imperfect, for social mobility.

Discipline, punctuality, and respect for hierarchy were not accidental outcomes; they were intentional design goals. When information was scarce and access to knowledge limited, memorization was a rational strategy. When jobs were stable and linear, education that prepared students for known roles made sense.

The problem, therefore, is not that the system was wrong. The problem is that the world it was designed for no longer exists.

What once created efficiency now creates rigidity.

What once ensured fairness now amplifies anxiety.

What once rewarded obedience now suppresses curiosity.

Understanding this origin is essential—not to defend the past, but to avoid repeating the mistake of designing education for a world that is already disappearing.

Memorization in an age of information scarcity

For most of human history, information was not abundant. It was rare, guarded, and difficult to access.

Books were limited, and libraries were few. Teachers were often the only living source of knowledge a child could encounter. In such a world, the ability to retain information accurately was power. Memorization was not an educational shortcut; it was a survival skill.

Students who could remember formulae, dates, definitions, procedures, and texts carried knowledge with them because there was nowhere else to retrieve it from. In professions like medicine, law, engineering, and administration, recall mattered deeply. Forgetting information was not an inconvenience; it could be catastrophic.

Rote learning, therefore, emerged as a practical response to the realities of the time.

Classrooms emphasized repetition because repetition ensured retention. Examinations tested memory because memory demonstrated mastery. A "good student" could reproduce what had been taught with precision and speed. This system rewarded discipline, consistency, and mental endurance—qualities highly valued in stable, hierarchical societies.

Even culturally, memorization held respect. Sacred texts, poetry, mathematical tables, and historical narratives were passed down orally long before they were printed. To memorize was to honor knowledge. To forget was to lose it.

But memorization, by its nature, prioritizes answers over questions.

It trains the mind to store information, not to challenge it. It values correctness over curiosity. Over time, students learn that success lies in repeating what is known rather than exploring what is possible.

This limitation was acceptable when knowledge changed slowly. When textbooks remained relevant for decades. When professions followed predictable paths. In such a world, mastering existing information was enough to ensure competence and employability.

Today, however, we live in the opposite reality.

Information is no longer scarce; it is overwhelming. Facts are searchable within seconds. Algorithms retrieve answers faster than any human memory ever could. The value of education can no longer lie in what students remember, but in how they interpret, apply, question, and ethically use information.

Memorization is not useless, but it is no longer sufficient.

Yet many classrooms continue to operate as though scarcity still exists. Students are still evaluated on recall rather than reasoning. Exams still reward speed over depth. Learning still feels like storage instead of sense-making.

The system has not failed because memorization was wrong. It has failed because memorization was never meant to stand alone—and the world moved on while education stood still.

Discipline, obedience, and standardization

Beyond knowledge, traditional education was designed to shape behavior.

Schools were not only places of learning; they were institutions of social conditioning. Punctuality, silence, uniformity, and adherence to rules were not incidental expectations—they were core outcomes of the system. The classroom mirrored the workplace students were being prepared for: structured, hierarchical, and authority-driven.

Obedience, in this context, was not viewed negatively. It signified reliability.

Employers needed individuals who could follow instructions without constant supervision, respect seniority, and function within clearly defined roles. Governments needed citizens who understood order, rules, and civic discipline. Education became the training ground where these traits were cultivated early and consistently.

Standardization made this possible at scale.

Uniform curricula ensured that every student, regardless of location, received the same content. Timetables regulated attention. Bells signaled transitions. Seating arrangements discouraged disruption. Assessment systems ranked students to identify who could conform most effectively to expected standards.

For generations, this approach created functional systems.

It produced workers who could operate machines, manage records, and maintain processes. It enabled institutions to grow without chaos. It brought predictability to societies attempting rapid economic and infrastructural development.

In countries with limited resources and large populations, standardization also created a sense of fairness. Everyone studied the same syllabus. Everyone wrote the same exams. Success appeared measurable and objective.

But compliance, when overemphasized, carries a hidden cost.

Students learn to wait for instructions instead of initiating action. They hesitate to question authority, even when something feels wrong. Creativity becomes risky. Failure becomes shameful. Over time, learning shifts from curiosity to caution.

The system unintentionally teaches students that being "right" matters more than being thoughtful, and being obedient matters more than being original.

This was manageable when jobs rewarded conformity and long-term stability. When organizations valued loyalty over innovation. When careers followed linear paths.

Today, however, compliance alone is no longer a competitive advantage.

The modern world demands adaptability, critical thinking, ethical judgment, and the courage to question flawed systems. AI can follow rules perfectly. What it cannot replicate, at least not meaningfully, is human judgment, empathy, and moral reasoning.

A system designed to produce compliant workers struggles to nurture independent thinkers.

Yet many schools still equate discipline with silence, learning with obedience, and success with conformity. The result is a growing mismatch between what education produces and what society now requires.

Discipline is not the enemy. Structure still matters. But discipline without agency creates adults who wait for permission in a world that rewards initiative.

Marks, rankings, and meritocracy

As education systems expanded, they needed a way to decide who progressed and who did not.

Marks, grades, and rankings offered a simple solution. They translated learning into numbers, making comparisons efficient and seemingly objective. In societies with limited opportunities and overwhelming demand, this system brought order to chaos.

Meritocracy, as it was understood, relied on measurement.

The ones who scored higher were seen as more capable. Those who ranked lower were encouraged to try harder or to accept different paths. Examinations became gateways to higher education, employment, and social mobility. For many families, especially in developing economies, marks represented hope.

And in many cases, they delivered.

The examination system rewarded effort, consistency, and discipline. It offered students from modest backgrounds a chance to compete on a common platform. A high score could open doors that social privilege might otherwise keep closed. For decades, marks functioned as a relatively fair sorting mechanism.

However, over time, measurement began to replace meaning.

Learning slowly shifted from understanding concepts to scoring well. Students learned to optimize performance rather than explore ideas. Subjects were valued not for their relevance, but for their weight in exams. Coaching centres flourished, training students to predict questions instead of think critically.

Marks became identity.

A student was no longer curious, creative, or thoughtful—they were a "topper" or an "average student." Self-worth became entangled with numbers. Failure, instead of being a learning signal, became a source of shame.

The system also overlooked important truths.

Not all abilities can be assessed through timed, written formats. Emotional AI, creativity, collaboration, ethical reasoning, and adaptability—skills increasingly essential in modern life—rarely translate into marks. Yet education continued to reward what was easiest to measure rather than what mattered most.

What once promoted fairness now fuels anxiety.

In an age where artificial AI can solve standardized problems instantly, evaluating human potential through repetitive testing becomes increasingly questionable. The question is no longer who can recall or apply known solutions, but who can frame problems, interpret ambiguity, and make value-based decisions.

Marks still have a place—but they cannot be the meaning of education.

When measurement becomes the goal, learning becomes shallow. And when rankings define worth, education loses its humanity.

The illusion of job security

For much of the twentieth century, education came with an unspoken promise.

Study well. Get good marks. Secure a degree. And life would follow a predictable path.

Education was seen as a direct pipeline to employment. Degrees aligned with professions. Skills remained relevant for decades. Organizations valued stability, loyalty, and long-term service. In return, employees received steady income, social status, and a sense of security.

This promise was not entirely false.

Teachers, engineers, doctors, bankers, and civil servants built entire careers on a single qualification. Families invested heavily in education because it reliably improved life outcomes. The system worked because the economy itself was stable and slow to change.

Education prepared students for known futures.

But the world changed.

Technological acceleration, globalization, and now artificial AI have dismantled the idea of permanent roles. Skills expire faster than degrees. Entire professions emerge and disappear within a decade. The relationship between education and employment has fractured.

Yet the education system continues to sell the old promise.

Students are still told that marks will secure their future. Parents still believe that the "right degree" ensures stability. Institutions still structure curricula around outdated job roles. When reality fails to match expectation, frustration and anxiety follow.

The illusion of job security is perhaps the most dangerous legacy of the traditional system.

It encourages students to optimize for credentials instead of capabilities. It discourages risk-taking and lifelong learning. It creates fear of change in a world where change is inevitable.

Artificial AI does not eliminate jobs—it reshapes them. But education that prepares students for fixed outcomes leaves them unprepared for fluid realities.

The future belongs not to those with perfect qualifications, but to those who can learn, unlearn, and adapt.

CHAPTER 2

WHAT THE TRADITIONAL SYSTEM GAVE US – AND WHERE IT FALLS SHORT TODAY

Education as a tool for nation-building

Years after independence, education carried a responsibility that was far greater than individual success. It was a tool for nation-building.

Countries emerging from colonial rule or economic hardship needed a shared identity, common language, and collective purpose. Schools became spaces where national values were transmitted, civic responsibilities were taught, and a sense of belonging was cultivated. Uniform curricula were not merely academic choices; they were political and social necessities.

Education helped stitch diverse populations into a functioning whole.

Textbooks standardized history, geography, and civic understanding. Language education enabled communication across various regions. Science and mathematics fueled industrial growth. Teacher authority reinforced social order during periods of rapid change. The classroom became one of the few places where children from different backgrounds encountered a shared narrative.

Standardized narratives leave little room for multiple perspectives. Uniform expectations ignore diverse learning needs. What once unified society now risks flattened human potential.

As nations mature, their educational goals must evolve.

Education can no longer focus solely on producing compliant citizens or efficient workers. It must prepare individuals to think independently, engage ethically, and contribute creatively.

The challenge is not to abandon education's role in nation-building, but to redefine what building a nation means in an interconnected, AI-driven world.

Teacher authority and classroom order

Traditional classrooms were built on a clear and deliberate hierarchy.

The teacher stood at the centre—not merely as an instructor, but as an authority figure. Knowledge flowed in one direction. Discipline was enforced. Expectations were unambiguous. In environments where large numbers of students had to be educated with limited resources, this structure was not optional—it was essential.

In classrooms with forty or more students, structure ensured that learning could take place effectively. Rules minimized chaos. Routines created predictability. Respect for the teacher maintained focus. For many students, especially those from unstable home environments, the classroom offered rare consistency.

This model also elevated the social role of teachers.

Teachers were seen as moral guides, custodians of knowledge, and community leaders. Their authority extended beyond academics into character formation. Parents trusted schools not just to teach, but to discipline and shape behaviour.

For decades, this clarity worked.

Students knew what was expected. Teachers knew their role. Schools functioned efficiently within their constraints. The system prioritized coverage of content and maintenance of order—both necessary in large-scale education systems.

Yet authority, when left unquestioned, can become limitation.

As knowledge expanded and diversified, the teacher-as-sole-expert model began to strain. No single individual could master every subject deeply. Students with different learning styles and questions found little space for dialogue. Curiosity often gave way to compliance.

The rise of digital access has further shifted this balance.

Students now encounter information beyond the classroom. They question more, compare sources, and challenge explanations. Authority based solely on position rather than facilitation struggles to remain relevant.

The issue is not that teacher authority is wrong. The issue is that authority must evolve from control to guidance.

In an AI-supported learning environment, teachers are no longer gatekeepers of information. They become mentors, sense-makers, and ethical anchors. Structure remains necessary, but it must support inquiry rather than suppress it.

Standardized curriculum and examinations

The traditional education system had one of its greatest achievements and that was its ability to function at scale.

When millions of students needed to be educated with limited resources be it the number of teachers, infrastructure, etc. standardization became a necessity. A common curriculum ensured students, regardless of the region, studied the same core subjects. Standardized examinations created a shared benchmark for evaluation.

This brought a sense of fairness.

Students from small towns could compete with those from the large cities, marks offered a visible, comparable metric. Higher education institutions could make selection decisions efficiently. Employers could rely on qualifications as signals of competence.

Clear syllabi, fixed assessment patterns, and uniform grading limited subjectivity. Success depended on effort and discipline rather than personal bias. For many first-generation learners, this predictability provided a rare sense of control over the future.

The system, however, rewarded sameness.

It assumed that all learners should move at the same pace, absorb content in the same way, and demonstrate understanding through the same formats. While this approach simplified administration, it ignored cognitive, emotional, linguistic, and cultural differences.

Students who did not fit the standard; creative thinkers, late bloomers, neurodiverse learners, often struggled not because they lacked ability, but because the system could not recognize it. Talent outside textbook performance remained invisible.

In an AI-driven world, the tension becomes even clearer.

Technology enables personalization at scale, yet many systems remain locked into uniform delivery. Examinations continue to prioritize speed and recall over reasoning and collaboration. What once ensured fairness now risks inequity.

Fairness today cannot mean treating everyone the same. It means giving each learner what they need to succeed.

Stability, predictability, and social mobility.

For generations, education functioned as a ladder.

Each rung was clearly marked—primary school, secondary school, higher education, employment. Progress was linear. Expectations were well defined. Families understood the path, even if the climb was difficult.

In uncertain economic environments, education offered structure and hope. It promised that effort would be rewarded, that discipline could overcome circumstance. For many, especially those from marginalized backgrounds, education was the only reliable pathway to social mobility.

Degrees signaled readiness. Institutions conferred legitimacy. Employers trusted qualifications. Stability was the reward for persistence.

Industries evolved slowly. Career paths were clear. Skills remained relevant over long periods. Education aligned neatly with employment, reinforcing trust in the system.

But ladders assume that the destination remains fixed.

In today's world, roles change faster than curricula. Skills become obsolete within years. Careers zigzag rather than ascend. The ladder metaphor no longer reflects reality.

Yet education continues to operate as though predictability still exists.

Students are trained for certainty in an age of volatility. They are prepared for known answers in a world defined by ambiguity. When reality disrupts the ladder, the system offers little guidance.

Social mobility, too, has stalled.

Access to education has expanded, but outcomes remain unequal. Standardized systems reward those who already possess resources—coaching, technology, exposure. The ladder exists, but its lower rungs are increasingly unstable.

Education must now prepare learners not just to climb, but to navigate shifting terrain.

When strengths become limitations

Every system carries within it the seeds of both success and stagnation.

The very strengths that made traditional education effective; structure, standardization, authority, predictability, become limitations when the context changes. What once enabled scale now restricts flexibility. What once ensured fairness now overlooks diversity. What once offered stability now creates fragility.

The problem is not that the system failed. The problem is that it refused to evolve at the pace of the world.

As technology accelerated, education responded slowly. As societies diversified, curricula remained narrow. As knowledge exploded, classrooms continued to prioritize coverage over understanding. As artificial AI emerged, systems still measured success using tools designed for scarcity and certainty.

Students feel disengaged and anxious. Teachers feel overburdened and constrained. Employers struggle to find adaptable talent. Schools face increasing pressure to justify relevance.

Most critically, education risks losing trust. When families invest years of effort without meaningful outcomes, disillusionment follows. When students sense that schooling prepares them for exams rather than life, motivation erodes. When teachers are forced to deliver outdated models, professional fulfillment declines.

Yet this moment also carries opportunity.

The foundations of traditional education—its commitment to access, discipline, and social good, can support transformation if reimagined thoughtfully. The goal is not replacement, but renewal.

Educationhastomovefromuniformitytopersonalization, from control to mentorship, from prediction to possibility.

The question no longer remains whether the system needs change. The question is whether leaders have the courage to preserve what matters while redesigning what no longer serves.

Case Study: Balancing Tradition and Technology in the Classroom

Background

St. Jude's Academy is a school that has long relied on traditional education methods, such as lecture-based teaching, physical textbooks, and manual grading. While these methods have fostered strong teacher-student interaction and developed students' interpersonal skills, the school has struggled with large class sizes and the limited ability to personalize lessons for every student's pace.

The Challenge

Teachers at the academy found it difficult to provide immediate feedback to all students due to the time-consuming nature of manual grading. Additionally, some students felt left behind by the fixed curriculum, while others felt unchallenged by its pace.

The Intervention: Introducing AI Tools

The school decided to adopt a blended approach, integrating AI-driven tools into their existing framework:

- Adaptive Learning Platforms: These tools provided tailored learning paths, allowing students to progress at their own individual pace.
- AI Tutors: Virtual assistants were made available to provide 24/7 support and remote learning options, making education more accessible.
- Automated Administrative Tasks: AI took over grading and resource management, freeing up teachers to focus on mentorship and complex student needs.

https://www.ijfmr.com/papers/2024/4/24635.pdf

CHAPTER 3

REIMAGINING EDUCATION IN AN AI WORLD – OPPORTUNITIES AND CHALLENGES

Why AI is not a threat

Whenever a powerful new technology emerges, society often reacts with fear before fully understanding its potential. Artificial AI is the same. Headlines warn of machines, replacing teachers, students cheating with algorithms, and schools becoming obsolete. These fears are understandable but they are misplaced.

AI is not a threat; it is a mirror that reveals the strengths, weaknesses, and unresolved contradictions of the system we already have.

If education were true about understanding, curiosity, and ethical reasoning, AI would enhance it. If education were already learner-centric, AI would personalize it. If assessment genuinely measured thinking, AI would deepen feedback rather than enable shortcuts.

The main reason we feel discomfort is because AI exposes what education has been avoiding.

For decades, schools have prioritized content delivery over sense-making. AI now delivers content better in terms of recalling instead of memorizing. It recognises patterns flawlessly.

This realization is unsettling because it forces a hard question: If a machine can outperform students in most school tasks, what exactly are we preparing students for?

The answer cannot be "better memorization" or "faster recall." Those battles are already lost—and rightly so.

AI challenges education to redefine its purpose.

Instead of asking how schools can protect themselves from AI, leaders must ask how education can focus on what cannot be automated: judgment, ethics, creativity, empathy, contextual thinking, and the ability to ask meaningful questions.

In this sense, AI becomes an ally. It frees teachers from repetitive tasks. It surfaces learning gaps early. It adapts content to individual pace. But most importantly, it exposes the gap between learning and schooling.

If students use AI to complete assignments without understanding, the failure is not technological, it is pedagogical. If assessments collapse in the presence of AI, it means they were never measuring deep learning to begin with.

AI does not erode academic integrity. It reveals where integrity was already fragile.

The real threat, therefore, is not artificial AI, but educational stagnation.

Systems that cling to outdated definitions of learning will struggle. Systems that evolve will thrive. The choice is not between humans and machines, but between obsolete education and meaningful education.

Reimagining education in an AI world begins with this shift in mindset: AI is not here to replace teachers or learners. It is here to demand that education finally become what it always claimed to be.

What is actually changing in classrooms

Artificial AI is often spoken about in abstract terms, but its impact on education is already tangible.

Classrooms may still look familiar—blackboards, desks, timetables, but beneath the surface, learning processes are beginning to shift. AI is not arriving as a single dramatic disruption; it is entering quietly, through tools that adapt, recommend, analyze, and assist.

One of the most significant changes is personalization.

AI-driven platforms can track how individual students learn, where they struggle, and how quickly they progress. Content adjusts in real time. Practice becomes targeted rather than repetitive. Students no longer have to move at the same pace simply because the timetable demands it. This challenges one of the oldest assumptions of schooling, that learning must be synchronized.

AI also alters the role of feedback. Traditionally, feedback arrived late and often felt final. Exams return weeks after learning has moved on. AI-enabled systems provide immediate responses, allowing students to reflect and improve while the learning moment is still alive. Mistakes become part of the process rather than a permanent judgment.

Teachers, too, experience change. Administrative tasks like, grading objective assessments, tracking attendance, analyzing performance data, can be automated. This does not diminish the teacher's role; it reclaims time. Time that can be redirected toward mentorship, discussion, and relationship-building.

However, these shifts also expose tensions.

When AI delivers content efficiently, teachers must redefine their value beyond information delivery. When students receive personalized pathways, schools must rethink uniform pacing and assessment. When data becomes central, ethical questions around privacy and bias emerge.

Classrooms are no longer just spaces of instruction; they become environments of data, choice, and interaction. Without thoughtful leadership, technology risks amplifying existing inequities. With intentional design, it can become a powerful equalizer.

The change, therefore, is not merely technological. It is cultural.

AI forces schools to confront long-standing questions:

What is the purpose of a lesson?

What does progress really mean?

How do we balance efficiency with humanity?

These are not questions AI can answer, but they are questions AI makes impossible to ignore.

Opportunities of AI in school education

The true potential of artificial AI in education lies not in speed or automation, but in possibility.

When thoughtfully integrated, AI has the capacity to address some of education's most persistent challenges—challenges that traditional systems have struggled to resolve at scale.

One of the most powerful opportunities is personalized learning.

Every classroom contains learners with different abilities, interests, backgrounds, and emotional states. Traditional systems respond by teaching to the middle, unintentionally neglecting both those who need more support and those who need greater challenge. AI enables differentiation without segregation. Students can learn at their own pace while remaining part of a shared learning community.

Another opportunity lies in access and reach.

Geography, language, and economic constraints have long limited educational opportunity. AI-powered tools can translate content, adapt materials for different learning needs, and bring high-quality resources to underserved regions. While technology alone cannot solve access inequities, it can significantly lower barriers when supported by policy and infrastructure.

AI also enhances teacher effectiveness. By analyzing patterns in student learning, AI can help teachers identify misconceptions early, design targeted interventions, and reflect on instructional strategies. This shifts teaching from reactive to proactive. Teachers gain insight not just into what students scored, but into how they think.

Beyond academics, AI opens space for holistic development. When routine tasks are automated, classrooms can devote more time to discussion, creativity, collaboration, and ethical reasoning. Learning expands beyond content mastery into meaning-making and application.

However, opportunity does not guarantee impact. Without clear purpose, AI risks becoming another layer of complexity. Without training, teachers may feel replaced rather than empowered. Without ethical safeguards, data-driven systems may reinforce bias rather than reduce it.

The promise of AI is not that it will fix education, but that it will force education to confront what truly matters.

Efficiency is only the beginning. The real opportunity lies in using AI to humanize learning, not mechanize it.

Challenges of AI integration

While artificial AI holds immense promise, its integration into education is neither simple nor risk-free.

Every technological shift carries unintended consequences, and education—deeply human and deeply unequal, magnifies them.

One of the most pressing challenges is equity. AI thrives on data and access. Schools with strong infrastructure, trained staff, and reliable connectivity benefit first. Under-resourced schools risk falling further behind, widening the very gaps education seeks to close. If AI becomes a privilege rather than a public good, inequality will deepen rather than diminish.

Equity is not only about access to devices, but about meaningful use. Students need guidance to engage with

AI as a learning tool rather than a shortcut. Teachers need training to integrate AI thoughtfully. Without this, technology may amplify dependence rather than understanding.

Ethics present another critical challenge. AI systems learn from data—and data reflects human bias. Algorithms can unintentionally reinforce stereotypes, disadvantage certain groups, or misinterpret learning behaviors. Issues of privacy, consent, and surveillance emerge when student data becomes a commodity.

Education cannot afford ethical ambiguity.

Schools must ask hard questions:

Who owns student data?

How transparent are AI systems?

What decisions should never be automated?

Perhaps the most underestimated challenge is teacher adaptation. Teachers are expected to adopt new tools while managing existing responsibilities. Without professional support, AI can feel threatening rather than empowering. Resistance often stems not from unwillingness, but from uncertainty and overload.

Technology changes faster than institutions. Human adaptation takes time.

If AI is introduced as a mandate rather than a partnership, it will fail. If teachers are positioned as facilitators of meaning rather than operators of tools, AI can become an ally.

The challenge, therefore, is not technological, it is leadership-driven.

How schools introduce AI will determine whether it becomes a force for growth or division.

NEP 2020 and the AI imperative

India's engagement with artificial AI in education does not begin from a blank slate. It is shaped by the vision articulated in the National Education Policy 2020, which quietly but decisively shifts the purpose of schooling.

NEP 2020 acknowledges a reality long ignored: the future cannot be predicted with certainty. Instead of training students for fixed roles, education must prepare them with capabilities that endure.

Critical thinking, creativity, ethical reasoning, flexibility, and lifelong learning sit at the heart of the policy. These are not technological goals; they are human ones. AI enters this framework not as a driver, but as an enabler.

The policy's emphasis on competency-based learning aligns naturally with AI-supported personalization. Its push for multidisciplinary education challenges subject silos that AI itself renders obsolete. Its focus on teacher empowerment recognizes that technology without human leadership is ineffective.

Importantly, NEP 2020 positions teachers as mentors and facilitators, not content transmitters. This shift is essential in an AI-enabled environment where information is abundant but understanding is scarce.

However, policy vision alone is insufficient.

India's diversity presents unique challenges. Vast differences in infrastructure, language, teacher preparedness, and student access mean that AI integration must be contextual, not uniform. A one-size-fits-all approach risks deepening inequality.

NEP 2020 implicitly demands thoughtful leadership.

School leaders must interpret the policy not as a checklist, but as a compass. AI should serve pedagogical intent, not drive it. Technology must adapt to classrooms, not classrooms to technology.

The Indian context also brings ethical responsibility.

As one of the world's largest education systems, India's choices will influence global practice. How AI is adopted, whether inclusively or selectively, will shape not just outcomes, but values.

The policy offers direction. AI offers tools. Leadership determines impact.

AI for personalised learning in Indian schools

In several urban and semi-urban school systems, AI-powered learning platforms have been introduced to support mathematics and language learning. These tools assess a student's current level, identify gaps, and adjust the difficulty of content accordingly. Instead of moving through chapters at a fixed pace, students progress based on mastery.

The immediate impact is visible.

Students who previously struggled are no longer left behind by the class timetable. They receive additional practice in areas of difficulty without public comparison or stigma. At the same time, advanced learners are challenged beyond the standard syllabus, reducing boredom and disengagement.

Teachers report a subtle but important shift.

Instead of spending most of their time explaining the same concept repeatedly, they are able to focus on small-group discussions, conceptual clarification, and individual mentoring. Data dashboards highlight which students need attention, allowing teachers to intervene early rather than after exam failure.

However, the case study also reveals limitations.

Schools that treated AI as a replacement for teaching saw little improvement. Where platforms were used mechanically, without integration into classroom pedagogy, learning gains plateaued. Students learned to "game" the system, clicking through tasks without reflection.

The most effective implementations shared common features:

- Teachers were trained not just in using tools, but in interpreting learning data
- AI was positioned as support, not authority
- Classroom discussions complemented digital practice
- Assessment was redesigned to value understanding, not platform completion

Perhaps the most important lesson was cultural.

When students understood why AI tools were being used, to support their learning rather than monitor them, engagement increased. When parents were involved and informed, trust improved.

This case demonstrates a crucial truth: AI does not personalize learning on its own. Educators do. Technology amplifies intent. Where intent is unclear, outcomes are shallow.

Balancing technology and mentorship

Technology changes systems. Leadership changes culture.

In the context of AI-enabled education, the role of school leadership becomes pivotal. Without clear vision and ethical grounding, even the most advanced tools can erode trust, deepen inequality, or reduce learning to metrics.

Effective leaders understand that AI must never replace human connection.

The most successful schools approach technology as an extension of mentorship, not a substitute for it. Leaders set clear expectations: AI supports learning, teachers guide meaning, and students remain active participants rather than passive recipients.

This balance begins with purpose. Leaders must articulate why AI is being introduced. Is it to reduce workload, personalize learning, improve equity, or enhance understanding? When purpose is explicit, resistance decreases and alignment improves.

Professional development is equally critical. Teachers need time, trust, and training to adapt. Leadership that frames AI as empowerment rather than surveillance, builds confidence. Teachers are more willing to experiment when failure is treated as learning rather than incompetence.

Leaders also serve as ethical stewards.

They must safeguard student data, ensure transparency in decision-making, and establish boundaries around automation. Not every educational decision should be data-driven. Judgment, empathy, and context still matter.

Perhaps most importantly, leaders model learning.

When school heads engage with AI thoughtfully: asking questions, reflecting publicly, and acknowledging uncertainty, they create a culture where adaptation feels safe. This signals that growth is expected not just from students, but from adults as well.

In an AI-driven world, leadership is less about control and more about coherence. Technology may shape the environment, but leadership shapes the experience.

Rethinking education in an AI world

Reimagining education in the age of artificial AI requires more than new tools. It demands reflection, especially from those responsible for shaping learning environments.

The following questions are not meant to offer quick answers. They are intended to provoke thoughtful dialogue among educators, leaders, and policymakers.

- If information is universally accessible, what should schools prioritize teaching?
- How can assessment measure understanding rather than output in an AI-enabled world?
- In what ways can AI support teachers without diminishing their professional agency?
- How do schools ensure that technology reduces, rather than widens, equity gaps?
- What ethical boundaries must be non-negotiable when student data is involved?
- How can leadership balance innovation with care, efficiency with humanity?

These questions shift the conversation from whether AI belongs in education to how education must change because of it.

The future of schooling will not be decided by algorithms alone. It will be shaped by the values, courage, and clarity of those who lead it.

CHAPTER 4

FROM INFORMATION TO UNDERSTANDING

When knowing is no longer enough

For many years, education revolved around a simple assumption, those who knew more would succeed.

Knowledge was scarce, making it powerful. Access to information determined opportunity. Schools existed to transmit what few possessed to many who did not. To be educated meant to know.

But today, information is everywhere. Facts are searchable in seconds. Tutorials, lectures, and explanations are in abundance. Students carry more information in their pockets than entire libraries once held.

Yet learning outcomes have not improved proportionally.

This contradiction reveals a deeper truth: information alone does not create understanding. Knowing a fact is different from understanding its implications. Recalling a formula is not the same as applying it meaningfully.

Access to content does not guarantee insight, judgment, or wisdom.

In an AI-enabled world, this distinction becomes unavoidable. If machines can retrieve, summarize, and even explain information, then education must move beyond what students know to how they think. The value of learning should shift from accumulation to interpretation.

Understanding requires seeing relationships between ideas, questioning assumptions, and applying knowledge in unfamiliar contexts. It demands time, reflection, and dialogue, elements often sacrificed in content-heavy curricula.

Traditional schooling often mistakes coverage for comprehension. Students rush through chapters without internalizing meaning. Assessment rewards recall rather than reasoning. The result is fragile learning—easily forgotten and rarely transferable.

The challenge is not the abundance of information, but the absence of sense-making.

Education must now help learners navigate complexity, ambiguity, and uncertainty. This requires a fundamental shift in pedagogy, assessment, and classroom culture.

When knowing is no longer enough, understanding becomes the new currency of education.

From memorization to meaning

Memorization has long been treated as the foundation of learning. In many classrooms, it still dominates because systems are built around it.

In an information-rich world, this reliance becomes increasingly problematic.

Memorization focuses on what to think. Understanding focuses on how and why.

When students memorize, they store isolated facts. When they seek meaning, they connect ideas, question relevance, and apply knowledge across contexts. This shift fundamentally changes the learner's relationship with content.

Meaning-making is slower than memorization, and it is also deeper.

Students must wrestle with concepts, confront confusion, and revise understanding. This process cannot be rushed or standardized easily. It demands classroom cultures that tolerate uncertainty and value inquiry over immediate correctness.

However, traditional education often penalizes struggle.

Mistakes are marked down. Questions that deviate from the syllabus are discouraged. Time pressure pushes teachers to "finish the portion" rather than explore ideas fully. In such environments, students learn to memorize not because it is effective, but because it is safe.

AI intensifies this tension.

If students can instantly retrieve answers, memorization becomes irrelevant. But without guidance, access to AI tools can also short-circuit thinking. Students may accept generated responses without analysis, mistaking fluency for understanding.

This reinforces an urgent need for pedagogical redesign.

Teachers must explicitly teach students how to evaluate information, ask better questions, and reflect on learning. Assignments must shift from reproducing content to interpreting it. Assessment must reward reasoning, not replication.

Meaning emerges when learners are invited to think.

This requires trust in students' capacity to engage deeply, and in teachers' ability to facilitate rather than dictate learning. It also requires leadership willing to prioritize depth over speed.

Education that clings to memorization in an AI world risks becoming performative rather than transformative.

The role of teachers in the age of learning

When information was scarce, teachers were valued primarily as transmitters of knowledge. Their expertise lay in what they knew and how clearly they could explain it.

In an age of abundance, this role must evolve.

Teachers are no longer the primary source of information, but they remain the primary source of meaning. Their value lies not in delivering answers, but in helping students make sense of complexity.

This shift is subtle but profound. Instead of asking, "Have I covered the syllabus?", teachers begin to ask, "Have students understood why this matters?" Instead of measuring success by silence and note-taking, classrooms become spaces of dialogue, questioning, and exploration.

Teachers in the age of understanding function as learning designers.

They craft experiences that provoke thinking. They pose problems rather than provide solutions. They guide students through confusion rather than rushing toward clarity. They create conditions where understanding can emerge.

This role requires new forms of expertise. Facilitating discussion, encouraging reflection, and responding to diverse perspectives demand emotional AI and pedagogical skill. Teachers must learn to read classrooms not just for compliance, but for engagement.

AI can support this transition. By handling routine tasks and providing data on student progress, AI frees teachers to focus on relational and intellectual mentorship. But this potential is realized only when teachers are trusted and supported.

If teachers are evaluated solely on test scores, the system discourages depth. If professional development prioritizes tools over pedagogy, technology overwhelms rather than empowers.

The age of understanding does not diminish teachers. It elevates them.

But this elevation requires systemic change—new expectations, new assessments, and new forms of leadership.

Pedagogies that build understanding

Understanding does not emerge from listening alone. It grows through engagement.

Traditional instruction emphasizes explanation. Teachers speak, students listen, and learning is assumed to occur. While explanation has its place, it rarely leads to deep understanding by itself.

Inquiry-based pedagogy reverses this logic.

Instead of beginning with answers, it begins with questions. Instead of presenting concepts fully formed, it invites students to explore, test, and reflect. Learning becomes an active process rather than a passive reception.

Several pedagogical approaches support this shift.

Project-based learning situates knowledge within real-world contexts. Students investigate problems that do not have single correct answers, integrating multiple disciplines and perspectives. Understanding develops through application.

Inquiry-based learning encourages curiosity. Students learn to frame questions, seek evidence, and construct arguments. The emphasis shifts from correctness to reasoning.

Collaborative learning recognizes that understanding is often social. Through discussion and debate, students encounter alternative viewpoints and refine their thinking. Learning becomes collective rather than competitive.

Reflection and metacognition make thinking visible. When students articulate what they understand and where they struggle, they develop awareness of their own learning processes. This self-knowledge is essential for lifelong learning.

These approaches demand time and flexibility.

They challenge rigid timetables and content-heavy syllabi. They require teachers to relinquish some control and trust the learning process. They also require assessment systems that value process as much as outcome.

In an AI-enabled classroom, inquiry becomes even more critical.

When answers are easily accessible, the ability to ask meaningful questions distinguishes deep learning from superficial engagement. Pedagogy must therefore prioritize sense-making over solution-finding.

Designing classrooms for understanding

Traditional classrooms were designed for efficiency. Rows of desks face a single focal point. Time is divided into fixed periods. Silence signals attention. This design reflects an instructional model where information flows in one direction.

An understanding-driven classroom looks different.

Physical space becomes flexible. Desks move. Students work in groups, circles, or independently as needed. The teacher moves among learners rather than standing apart. The environment signals that learning is active, collaborative, and evolving.

Deep understanding cannot always be confined to forty-minute blocks. Some concepts require sustained engagement. Inquiry unfolds unevenly. Reflection takes time. Schools committed to understanding allow flexibility within schedules, creating space for exploration and synthesis.

Culture may be the most important design element. Classrooms that value understanding normalize questions and uncertainty. Mistakes are treated as learning opportunities rather than failures. Curiosity is encouraged. Students feel safe to express incomplete ideas and revise their thinking.

Adaptive tools allow students to engage with content at their own pace, freeing classroom time for discussion and application. Data insights help teachers identify where understanding is fragile, guiding targeted support.

However, no technology can compensate for a culture that prioritizes speed over depth.

Designing classrooms for understanding requires intentional leadership. Policies, assessments, and expectations must align with pedagogical goals. Without this coherence, innovation remains superficial.

Leadership in the age of understanding

Shifting from information delivery to understanding requires more than classroom-level change. It demands leadership willing to rethink long-standing assumptions about efficiency, coverage, and success.

In many education systems, speed is mistaken for effectiveness. Syllabi are dense. Timelines are rigid. Teachers feel pressure to "finish" content rather than ensure comprehension. Leaders, often evaluated on short-term metrics, reinforce this pace unintentionally.

Effective leaders create conditions where depth is valued over speed. They recognize that meaningful learning may appear slower but yields more durable outcomes. They support teachers in experimenting with pedagogy without fear of penalty.

This requires courage. Leaders must be willing to question traditional indicators of success. They must engage parents in conversations about why learning may look different. They must advocate for assessment reforms that align with understanding rather than recall.

AI adds both opportunity and pressure.

Data dashboards can tempt leaders to focus on easily measurable outcomes. Used wisely, data informs reflection and improvement. Used narrowly, it reduces learning to numbers.

When leaders ask reflective questions, model learning, and prioritize ethical considerations, they signal that understanding matters. When they reward innovation and collaboration, they foster a culture of growth.

Ethics, judgment, and meaning in AI-supported learning

As artificial AI becomes more embedded in learning environments, the distinction between knowing and understanding takes on ethical significance.

AI systems can generate answers, recommend actions, and simulate reasoning. But they do not possess values, conscience, or moral judgment. These qualities remain distinctly human—and education must actively cultivate them.

Understanding is inseparable from ethics. When students evaluate information, they must consider source, bias, and consequence. When they apply knowledge, they must weigh impact. When they make decisions, they must reflect on values.

AI can support analysis, but it cannot replace responsibility.

Without ethical grounding, learners may accept AI outputs uncritically. They may mistake confidence for correctness. They may outsource judgment to systems designed without full transparency.

Education must therefore teach students how to engage with AI thoughtfully. This includes questioning outputs, understanding limitations, and recognizing when human judgment is essential. Ethical education becomes not an add-on, but a core component of understanding.

Teachers play a central role here. By modeling reflective decision-making and discussing real-world dilemmas, teachers help students connect knowledge to values. Classrooms become spaces where ethical reasoning is practiced, not preached.

Policies should clarify acceptable use, protect privacy, and ensure transparency. More importantly, they should affirm that technology serves human purposes—not the other way around.

Framework , understanding the ecosystem

To move from information-rich schooling to understanding-driven education, isolated changes are insufficient. What is required is an ecosystem—an interconnected set of conditions that together support deep learning.

The Understanding Ecosystem rests on four interdependent pillars.

The first is **Pedagogy.** Teaching must prioritize inquiry, dialogue, application, and reflection. Lessons are designed not to deliver content, but to provoke thinking. Students engage with ideas actively rather than receive them passively.

The second is **Assessment.** Evaluation must measure reasoning, interpretation, and growth. Feedback becomes formative and ongoing. Mistakes are signals for learning rather than final judgments. AI can support timely feedback, but human interpretation remains central.

The third is **Environment**. Classrooms, schedules, and cultures must support exploration. Physical and psychological safety enable risk-taking. Flexibility in time and space allows understanding to develop organically.

The fourth is **Leadership.** Leaders align vision, policy, and practice. They protect time for deep learning, support teacher development, and ensure ethical use of technology. Leadership sustains coherence across the system.

These pillars reinforce one another.

Pedagogical innovation without assessment reform creates frustration. Flexible environments without leadership clarity lead to inconsistency. Technology without ethical grounding undermines trust.

Understanding emerges when the ecosystem functions as a whole.

AI becomes a catalyst rather than a driver. Teachers become facilitators of meaning. Students become active constructors of knowledge.

Reflection questions

Leaders play a decisive role in shaping whether schools prioritize information or understanding. The following questions are intended to guide thoughtful reflection and dialogue.

- Do our curricula allow time for depth, or do they reward speed and coverage?
- How do our assessments signal what we truly value—recall or reasoning?
- In what ways are teachers supported to design learning experiences rather than deliver content?
- How does our use of AI enhance understanding rather than replace thinking?

- Are ethical reasoning and judgment explicitly taught and modeled?
- What cultural signals do our classrooms send about curiosity, mistakes, and inquiry?

CHAPTER 5

LEARNER-CENTRIC EDUCATION

Why uniformity no longer serves learners

Uniformity once made education possible at scale.

When systems were built to educate large populations with limited resources, standardization ensured order, fairness, and efficiency. Teaching everyone the same content, at the same pace, in the same way was not practical.

But now those systems have begun to limit growth.

Learners think differently about how they feel, how they process information, and how they engage with the world. Some grasp concepts visually, others through dialogue or application. Some move quickly, others need time. Some thrive in structure, others in exploration.

Uniform systems flatten these differences.

When all learners are expected to move together, many are left behind—not because they lack ability, but because the system cannot accommodate variation. Others become disengaged because learning feels disconnected from their interests and strengths.

In such environments, labels emerge.

"Slow learners," "average students," and "toppers" become identities rather than temporary states. Education begins to sort learners instead of supporting them.

The limitations of uniformity become even more visible in an AI-enabled world.

Technology allows personalization at scale, yet many systems remain locked into one-size-fits-all delivery. This mismatch creates frustration—for students, teachers, and families alike.

Learner-centric education does not reject structure. It redefines it.

Instead of uniform pathways, it offers flexible routes toward shared goals. Instead of standard pace, it emphasizes mastery. Instead of passive reception, it encourages agency.

Uniformity solved the problems of the past. Learner-centricity responds to the realities of the present.

Understanding Learner Diversity — Cognitive, Emotional, and Cultural

Learner-centric education begins with a simple but often overlooked truth: no two learners are the same.

Diversity in classrooms extends far beyond visible differences. It includes how students think, feel, communicate, and relate to learning itself. Traditional systems acknowledge diversity in principle, but rarely design for it in practice.

Cognitive diversity shapes how learners process information.

Some students grasp concepts quickly through abstract reasoning, while others need concrete examples or repeated application. Some excel in language, others in spatial or logical thinking. These differences are not deficits; they are variations in human AI.

Uniform instruction often treats these variations as problems to be corrected rather than strengths to be leveraged.

Emotional and social diversity influences engagement.

Students arrive in classrooms with different levels of confidence, anxiety, motivation, and support. Learning is deeply emotional. A system that ignores this dimension risks mistaking disengagement for incapacity.

Linguistic and cultural diversity further complicates the picture.

Students bring different languages, cultural references, and ways of meaning-making. When curricula reflect only dominant narratives, many learners struggle to see themselves in what they are taught.

Learner-centric education recognizes diversity as a resource.

Instead of asking how students can fit the system, it asks how the system can respond to students. This shift demands flexibility in pedagogy, assessment, and expectations.

AI can support this responsiveness by offering adaptive pathways and insights into learning patterns. But technology alone cannot replace empathy and professional judgment.

Personalized Learning in Practice — What It Really Means

Personalized learning is often misunderstood.

It is not about isolating learners behind screens. It is not about replacing teachers with algorithms and it is not about allowing students to learn "whatever they want" without structure.

At its core, personalized learning is about responsiveness.

It means adjusting pace, pathway, and support so that each learner can move toward shared learning goals in a way that aligns with their needs and strengths. The destination remains common; the routes vary.

In practice, personalization shows up in small but meaningful ways.

Students may receive different levels of support for the same concept. Some may work with concrete examples while others explore applications. Choice may exist in how learning is demonstrated—through writing, presentation, discussion, or creation.

Mastery replaces time as the primary measure of progress. Instead of moving on because the calendar demands it, learners move on because they understand. This reduces gaps and builds confidence. Struggle becomes part of learning rather than a sign of failure.

Teachers remain central to this process. Personalization does not eliminate structure; it requires intentional design. Teachers plan flexible activities, monitor progress, and intervene thoughtfully. AI tools can assist by providing data and adaptive practice, but human judgment guides decisions.

The goal is not customization for its own sake. Personalized learning aims to help learners develop agency—to understand how they learn, take ownership of growth, and engage with content meaningfully.

When done well, personalization does not fragment the classroom. It strengthens community by honoring difference within shared purpose.

From Instructor to Learning Partner

Learner-centric education redefines the relationship between teacher and student.

In traditional classrooms, the teacher directs learning. Content, pace, and assessment are largely predetermined. Students follow.

In learner-centric environments, the teacher becomes a learning partner. This does not diminish authority or expertise. It reframes it. Teachers guide, observe, question, and support. They respond to learners rather than prescribe identical paths for all.

The teacher's role shifts in several important ways.

From delivering information to **designing learning experiences.**

From controlling pace to **monitoring progress.**

From evaluating performance to **supporting growth.**

This role requires deep professional skill.

Teachers must interpret learner data, notice patterns, and respond flexibly. They must balance autonomy with structure. They must cultivate trust so students feel safe to take ownership of learning.

AI can assist, but it cannot replace this relational work.

Adaptive platforms may suggest next steps, but teachers decide how and when to intervene. Technology provides signals; teachers provide meaning.

This shift also demands systemic support.

Teachers cannot personalize learning in rigid systems that demand uniform pacing and standardized outcomes. Professional development, planning time, and leadership alignment are essential.

When teachers are positioned as partners rather than enforcers, learners engage more deeply. Responsibility is shared. Learning becomes collaborative rather than transactional.

Leveraging AI for Personalization

AI has the potential to make personalization practical at scale but only when it is used as a support system, not a substitute for human judgment.

In traditional classrooms, personalization depended almost entirely on individual teachers. With large class sizes and rigid schedules, tailoring learning to each student was often unrealistic. As a result, personalization remained an ideal rather than a reality.

AI changes this equation.

AI systems can analyze learning patterns, identify gaps, and suggest resources aligned with a learner's pace and needs. They can offer adaptive practice, instant feedback, and multiple representations of the same concept.

Personalization driven purely by algorithms risks narrowing learning into isolated skill optimization.

Education is more than efficiency. It is about curiosity, struggle, dialogue, and meaning-making.

This is why AI must remain assistive, not authoritative.

Teachers interpret AI-generated insights through a human lens. They decide when a learner needs challenge, reassurance, or redirection. They understand emotional readiness, motivation, and context—factors no system fully captures.

Used well, AI reduces routine burden.

It frees teachers from repetitive grading and content delivery so they can focus on mentoring, discussion, and deeper learning design.

Used poorly, it fragments learning and weakens human connection.

The goal is not hyper-individualization where each learner exists in isolation. The goal is personalized pathways within shared learning experiences.

When AI supports teachers rather than replaces them, personalization becomes both scalable and humane.

Curriculum Flexibility and Learner Choice

When every learner is expected to reach the same outcomes at the same time, choice becomes superficial. True learner-centric education requires flexibility by design, not as an exception.

Traditional curricula prioritize coverage. Topics are sequenced linearly, time-bound, and standardized. Learners move forward regardless of readiness or interest.

Learner-centric curricula prioritize progression. This does not mean abandoning standards. It means allowing multiple routes toward shared goals.

Flexibility appears in several ways.

Learners may choose projects that align with their interests while developing common competencies. They may progress at different paces, revisiting concepts without penalty. They may demonstrate understanding through varied formats—presentations, portfolios, prototypes, or reflective writing.

Choice increases engagement, but it also demands responsibility.

Students must learn to plan, reflect, and make decisions about their learning. These are not innate skills. They must be taught, scaffolded, and supported.

Teachers play a crucial role here. They help learners connect choices to long-term goals. They ensure rigor is maintained. They intervene when choice becomes avoidance rather than exploration.

AI can assist by mapping curriculum options, tracking competency progress, and suggesting pathways—but it cannot replace guidance.

Curriculum flexibility also challenges assessment structures. When learners move differently, assessment must shift from ranking to evidence of growth.

Without flexible curricula, learner-centric education becomes a slogan. With it, learning becomes purposeful and self-directed.

Assessment for Personalized Learning

Assessment is the silent driver of student behavior.

No matter how progressive a curriculum claims to be, learners ultimately focus on what is measured. If assessment rewards memorization and speed, personalization collapses into compliance.

Learner-centric education requires assessment to function as feedback, not judgment.

Traditional assessment systems compare learners against one another. They rank, sort, and label. This approach assumes uniform paths and timelines—conditions that personalization explicitly rejects.

Personalized learning demands a different logic.

Assessment must track individual growth over time rather than relative position. Progress is measured against clearly defined competencies, not against peers.

This shift changes both form and purpose.

Formative assessment becomes central. Feedback becomes continuous. Mistakes become data, not failure.

Learners are assessed when they are ready, not when the calendar demands it. They are given multiple opportunities to demonstrate understanding in diverse ways.

Teachers become assessors of learning process, not just outcomes.

AI can support this transition by capturing learning evidence, identifying patterns, and providing timely feedback. But final interpretation remains human.

Overreliance on automated scoring risks flattening complex learning into narrow metrics. Personalized assessment must honor creativity, reasoning, collaboration, and reflection—dimensions that resist simple quantification.

Most importantly, learners must be involved in assessment.

Self-assessment and reflection build metacognition. When learners understand what they are aiming for and how they are progressing, ownership deepens.

Assessment aligned with personalization does not lower standards. It makes standards reachable in different ways.

Equity in Learner-Centric Education

Personalization without equity risks becoming privilege.

When learner-centric models are implemented without intention, they can amplify existing advantages. Students with access to technology, guidance, and supportive environments benefit more quickly, while others fall further behind.

Equity must therefore be designed into personalization, not treated as an outcome.

Traditional systems often claim fairness through uniformity—everyone receives the same content, at the same pace, assessed in the same way. In reality, this approach ignores differences in readiness, language, context, and support.

Learner-centric education recognizes that fairness means providing what each learner needs to succeed, not providing the same experience to all.

This requires several deliberate choices.

Access to technology must be universal, reliable, and supported. Curricula must reflect cultural and linguistic diversity. Teachers must be trained to recognize and counter unconscious bias. Learning pathways must be flexible without becoming opaque or exclusive.

AI can help close gaps when used responsibly.

Adaptive tools can support learners who need more time or alternative explanations. Translation and accessibility features can reduce language and disability barriers. Data can help identify learners who are quietly disengaging.

But AI can also reinforce inequity if trained on biased data or deployed without oversight.

Equity demands transparency.

Learners and families should understand how learning decisions are made. Teachers should retain the authority to override automated recommendations when they conflict with context or judgment.

Leadership plays a crucial role here. Equity cannot be delegated to software or individual teachers. It must be a system-level commitment reflected in policy, resources, and accountability.

Learner-centric education succeeds only when personalization expands opportunity rather than concentrating it.

Leadership Strategies for Implementing Learner-Centric Education

Learner-centric education cannot be sustained through isolated classroom efforts.

Without aligned leadership, personalization remains fragmented—dependent on individual enthusiasm rather than institutional design.

Leaders set the conditions under which learner-centric models either flourish or fail.

The first responsibility of leadership is vision clarity.

Teachers and students must understand why personalization matters and how it connects to broader educational goals. Without a shared purpose, change feels like added workload rather than meaningful reform.

The second responsibility is structural alignment.

Timetables, assessment policies, curriculum frameworks, and reporting systems must support flexible learning. Rigid schedules and standardized pacing undermine even the most innovative classroom practices.

Leadership must also invest in capacity building.

Teachers need training not just in tools, but in pedagogy—data interpretation, mentoring, reflective assessment, and learning design. This requires time, trust, and ongoing professional support.

Technology decisions should follow educational intent, not trend. Leaders must ask:

Does this tool deepen learning?

Does it strengthen teacher-student relationships?

Does it promote equity?

Finally, leaders must model learner-centric behavior themselves.

When leadership listens, reflects, iterates, and learns openly, the culture shifts. Schools develop adaptive systems rather than compliance-driven organizations.

Learner-centric education is not a program to be implemented. It is a culture to be led.

Reflection questions for leaders

Learner-centric education requires leaders to examine not only systems, but assumptions.

The following reflections are designed to support thoughtful, context-sensitive action rather than quick implementation.

- Where in our system does uniformity still override learner needs, even unintentionally?
- How do our curriculum and assessment structures support—or restrict—personalized pathways?
- In what ways are teachers empowered to act as learning partners rather than content deliverers?
- How is AI currently used: to reduce workload and support learning, or to enforce efficiency and control?
- Which learners benefit most from personalization in our context—and who may be left behind?
- How do we ensure transparency and trust in AI-supported learning decisions?
- What leadership behaviors must change to sustain learner-centric practices over time?

These questions should be revisited as systems evolve, tools change, and learners grow.

Learner-centric education is not a destination. It is an ongoing commitment to responsiveness, equity, and purpose.

CHAPTER 6

TEACHERS AS MENTORS IN THE AI ERA – FROM CONTENT EXPERTS TO LEARNING LEADERS

The Evolving Role of Teachers

For most of modern education, the teacher's primary role was clear: transmit knowledge.

This made sense in a world where information was scarce, textbooks were limited, and teachers were the most reliable source of subject expertise. Authority came from knowing more than students.

That world no longer exists.

Today, information is abundant, searchable, and instantly accessible. AI systems can explain concepts, generate examples, and answer questions at scale. When teachers are positioned only as content providers, they are placed in direct competition with machines—and unfairly so.

The teacher's value now lies elsewhere.

In the AI era, teachers are not replaced; they are repositioned.

Their role shifts from delivering answers to shaping understanding. From controlling classrooms to cultivating learning environments. From covering syllabus to guiding growth.

This evolution is not a loss of authority. It is a deepening of purpose.

Teachers become mentors who help learners make sense of information, ask better questions, and connect learning to real life. They support emotional resilience, ethical reasoning, and self-belief—areas where technology has limits.

This role demands new competencies.

Teachers must interpret data without being ruled by it. They must balance structure with autonomy. They must engage learners not through instruction alone, but through relationship.

Importantly, this shift also requires institutional recognition.

If systems continue to evaluate teachers primarily on content delivery and exam results, mentorship remains invisible and undervalued.

Reimagining education means reimagining what it means to teach.

Mentorship Beyond Content

Mentorship in education has often been treated as an add-on, something informal, optional, or dependent on individual goodwill. In the AI era, mentorship becomes central, not peripheral.

When information is easily accessible, what learners need most is not more content, but guidance.

Mentorship extends learning beyond academics into areas that shape long-term success and well-being.

First, there is **academic guidance.**

Mentors help learners set goals, reflect on progress, and make sense of feedback. They support learners in navigating personalized pathways without feeling lost or overwhelmed. Rather than pushing performance, they cultivate direction.

Second, mentorship includes **social and emotional support.**

Learning is deeply emotional. Anxiety, self-doubt, comparison, and fear of failure influence engagement more than curriculum design. Teachers as mentors notice these signals. They normalize struggle and help learners build resilience.

Third, mentorship supports **career and purpose orientation.**

In a rapidly changing world, students need help connecting learning to possibilities. Mentors expose learners to diverse pathways, challenge narrow definitions of success, and encourage curiosity rather than premature specialization.

Finally, mentorship involves **ethical development.**

As learners use AI tools, mentors help them understand responsibility, integrity, and impact. They guide conversations about authorship, bias, and decision-making in ways no policy document can.

AI can assist mentorship by offering insights and reducing administrative load, but mentorship itself remains fundamentally human.

It is built on trust, presence, and understanding—qualities that cannot be automated.

Teachers as Learning Designers

As the teacher's role shifts from instruction to mentorship, another transformation follows naturally: teachers become designers of learning experiences.

In traditional systems, learning design is centralized. Curricula, textbooks, and assessments are predefined, leaving teachers to execute rather than create. This limits responsiveness and innovation.

In the AI era, effective learning requires intentional design.

Teachers curate resources, structure inquiry, and create conditions where understanding can emerge. They decide when learners should explore independently, collaborate, or receive direct guidance.

Designing learning means thinking beyond lessons.

It involves sequencing experiences that build curiosity, challenge assumptions, and encourage reflection. It means anticipating misconceptions and designing opportunities for learners to confront them.

AI expands the teacher's design capacity.

It can generate examples, simulations, and practice sets. It can suggest variations and track learner responses. But AI does not design meaning—it provides components.

Teachers assemble these components with purpose.

They ensure learning remains coherent, inclusive, and aligned with values. They adapt designs based on classroom dynamics, not just data outputs.

This role requires time and trust.

When teachers are overloaded with administrative tasks or constrained by rigid scripts, design becomes impossible. Systems must recognize learning design as core professional work, not an extra responsibility.

Professional Development for the AI Era

Expecting teachers to evolve without reimagining professional development is unrealistic.

Most existing training models focus on compliance: new policies, tools, or curricula, rather than growth. In the AI era, professional development must become continuous, contextual, and collaborative.

Teachers do not need to become technologists.

They need confidence in pedagogy, data interpretation, mentoring, and ethical decision-making. AI literacy matters, but only insofar as it strengthens teaching practice.

Effective professional development in the AI era has three defining features.

First, it is **practice-centered.**

Training is embedded in classroom realities, not abstract workshops. Teachers learn by designing lessons, testing approaches, and reflecting on outcomes.

Second, it is **peer-driven.**

Communities of practice allow teachers to share insights, challenges, and strategies. Learning from colleagues builds trust and relevance far more than top-down instruction.

Third, it is **iterative.**

As tools evolve, so must teacher understanding. Professional learning becomes a cycle of experimentation, feedback, and refinement rather than a one-time event.

Leadership plays a decisive role here.

Schools must allocate time for learning, reduce unnecessary administrative load, and signal that growth is valued over perfection.

AI can support professional development by offering personalized learning pathways for teachers themselves. But, as with students, technology must support—not replace—human learning.

Investing in teacher growth is not optional. It is the foundation of any meaningful educational transformation.

Integrating AI in teacher mentorship

AI enters classrooms most visibly through tools, but its deeper impact is felt through how it reshapes teacher time and attention.

When integrated thoughtfully, AI strengthens mentorship. When adopted carelessly, it distances teachers from learners.

The key distinction lies in intent.

AI should handle what is repeatable and administrative, allowing teachers to focus on what is relational and developmental.

For example, AI can:

- Track learner progress across competencies
- Identify patterns of disengagement or struggle

- Provide draft feedback or practice resources
- Manage routine documentation

These functions reduce cognitive load and free time for conversation, observation, and guidance.

However, mentorship cannot be automated.

AI may flag that a learner is falling behind, but it cannot understand why. It cannot sense confidence loss, family stress, or quiet resilience. Only teachers can contextualize data within lived experience.

This is where mentorship and AI intersect. Teachers interpret AI insights as signals, not decisions. They decide when to intervene, when to wait, and how to respond.

Ethical clarity is essential.

Learners should know how AI is used and why. Mentorship depends on trust, and opaque systems erode it quickly.

Teachers must also model responsible AI use.

Mentorship and Assessment

In mentorship-driven education, assessment is no longer an endpoint.

It becomes part of an ongoing conversation.

Traditional assessment positions teachers as judges. Learners submit work, teachers evaluate it, and feedback often arrives after the learning moment has passed. This creates distance rather than growth.

Mentorship reframes assessment as guided reflection.

Teachers help learners understand where they are, why they are there, and what comes next. Feedback is timely, specific, and oriented toward improvement rather than comparison.

This approach changes the tone of assessment.

Instead of asking, "What grade did I get?", learners ask, "What am I learning?"

AI can support this shift by providing rapid feedback and tracking progress across competencies. But feedback alone is not mentorship.

Teachers contextualize feedback.

They help learners interpret results, manage emotions, and set realistic goals. They recognize effort, not just outcomes.

Mentorship also requires assessment to be dialogic.

Learners participate in self-assessment and goal-setting. They articulate their thinking, reflect on mistakes, and take ownership of growth.

This builds metacognitive skill—one of the most valuable outcomes of education.

When assessment is embedded within mentorship, it stops being a source of fear and becomes a tool for clarity.

Leadership in teacher mentorship

Teacher mentorship does not thrive by individual effort alone. It requires intentional leadership.

When schools value teachers only for syllabus completion and exam results, mentorship becomes invisible and unsustainable. Leadership determines whether mentoring is treated as core work or optional goodwill.

Leaders must first **redefine success.**

If mentoring, relationship-building, and learner growth are not reflected in evaluation systems, teachers receive a clear message about priorities. Leadership must broaden indicators of success to include student well-being, engagement, and long-term development.

Second, leadership must create **structural support.**

Mentorship requires time—time for conversations, reflection, and follow-up. Overloaded schedules and administrative pressure erode mentoring capacity. Leaders must protect time for mentoring just as they protect instructional time.

Third, leaders must invest in **mentorship capability.**

Not all teachers are trained mentors by default. Professional learning should include coaching skills, emotional AI, listening, and ethical guidance—especially in AI-supported environments.

Fourth, leadership must model mentorship behaviors.

When leaders listen, provide feedback, and support teacher growth, they normalize a mentoring culture. Teachers mirror what leadership practices.

Finally, leadership must ensure **ethical alignment.**

Mentorship involves trust. Leaders must set clear boundaries around data use, AI deployment, and student privacy. Teachers should never feel pressured to prioritize metrics over human judgment.

Equity and mentorship

Mentorship without equity lens risks serving only those who already feel seen.

Many times, a student who is more confident, articulate, or well-supported naturally attracts more guidance. Those who struggle quietly, because of various reasons, often receive less attention.

Equitable mentorship should be intentional. Teachers need systems that help them notice every learner. AI can assist by highlighting patterns of disengagement or uneven progress, but equity depends on how teachers respond to these signals.

Mentorship for equity means meeting learners where they are.

Some students need academic direction, some need reassurance on structure or belief, and some need help navigating expectations that were never made explicit.

Teachers as mentors help decode the unspoken rules, norms, and pathways that advantage some learners over others.

Mentorship should respect learners' identity, languages, and lived experiences. Guidance that ignores context, however well-intentioned, can alienate rather than empower.

Schools should ensure manageable mentor-learner ratios, provide training on bias awareness, and allocate resources where need is greatest.

AI can widen access to support, but it must not replace human care. Algorithms cannot understand aspiration shaped by circumstance.

Framework

To move mentorship from intention to practice, schools need a clear, shared framework. Without one, mentoring depends on individual personality rather than systemic design.

A practical mentorship framework in the AI era rests on five interconnected pillars.

1. Relationship First

Trust is the foundation of mentorship. Teachers prioritize knowing learners—their strengths, anxieties, motivations, and contexts. AI data informs this understanding but never replaces human connection.

2. Guided Autonomy

Mentors help learners make choices without abandoning them to uncertainty. Students are supported to set goals, reflect, and adjust paths while knowing guidance is always available.

3. Feedback as Dialogue

Assessment becomes an ongoing conversation. Teachers use feedback to prompt reflection, not just correction. Learners are active participants in understanding their growth.

4. Ethical and Responsible use of AI

Teachers model discernment in using AI—questioning outputs, acknowledging limits, and reinforcing integrity. Mentorship includes helping learners use technology responsibly and thoughtfully.

5. Continuous Growth—for Learners and Teachers

Mentorship is dynamic. Teachers reflect on their own practice, seek feedback, and adapt as learners. This helps them to evolve with support of technology.

Reflection questions for leaders and educators

The transition from content delivery to mentorship requires deep reflection at both individual and institutional levels.

- How is mentorship currently recognized and supported in our system?
- What structures limit teachers' ability to mentor meaningfully?
- How do we balance AI efficiency with human judgment and care?
- Which learners receive the most mentorship attention—and which may be overlooked?
- How are teachers supported in developing mentoring skills over time?
- What leadership behaviors reinforce a mentoring culture?

Basingstoke College of Technology (United Kingdom)

In 2024-2025, this college implemented a suite of AI tools (Google Gemini and TeacherMatic) with a specific goal: Teacher Wellbeing and Mentorship.

- **The Problem:** Teachers were spending over 10 hours a week on lesson planning, resource creation, and administrative emails, leaving little energy for 1-on-1 student support.
- **The AI Intervention:** Teachers used AI to summarize meeting notes, draft parent letters, and generate customized practice questions based on specific student gaps.
- **The Mentorship Result:** An internal study showed teachers saved an average of 5.1 hours per week.

Instead of going home exhausted, they repurposed that time into targeted 1-on-1 interventions for students with special educational needs (SEND) and mental health challenges.

- **The "Learning Leader" Shift:** The teacher's role moved from "Admin Manager" to "Emotional Anchor," focusing on essential human skills like communication and resilience that the AI could not provide.

CHAPTER 7

CURRICULUM FOR AN UNKNOWN FUTURE – EDUCATING FOR POSSIBILITY, NOT PREDICTION

The need for a future-ready curriculum

Education has always prepared learners for the future. The only major difference today is that the future is no longer predictable.

Traditional curricula are built on assumption that we can find stable careers, fixed knowledge domains, and linear progressions. Schools prepare students for roles that existed earlier, using framework that were not designed for this age.

That very model is breaking down. Technological change, especially AI, is reshaping industries faster than curriculum cycles can respond. Skills have become obsolete and new rules are emerging without warning. Preparing learners for specific outcomes is no longer sufficient.

A future-ready curriculum therefore shifts its focus. Instead of preparing students for known roles, it prepares them to adapt.

This does not mean abandoning foundational knowledge. Literacy, numeracy, scientific reasoning, and historical understanding remain essential. But they are no longer endpoints. They are tools.

A future-ready curriculum emphasizes:

- Learning how to learn
- Critical thinking and sense making
- Creativity and problem framing
- Ethica judgement in complex situations

It values depth over coverage and understanding over recall.

Uncertainty becomes a design condition, not a flaw. Curricula must remain flexible, allowing revision as contexts change. This requires letting go of the illusion of control and embracing responsiveness.

The goal is to prepare learners to nevigate whatever future arrives.

Principles of a future-ready curriculum

A future-ready curriculum is not defined by subjects alone. It is shaped by principles that guide how learning is structured, experienced, and assessed.

The first principle is transferability.

Knowledge should be such that it is usable beyond the classroom. Learners should be able to apply concepts across contexts, disciplines, and problems. This requires teaching for understanding and not memorization.

The second principle is adaptability.

Curricula must allow for change: new content, emerging issues, and evolving tools. Fixed syllabi eventually becomes outdated. Modular structures and periodic review make adaptation possible without disruption.

The third principle is interdisciplinarity.

Real-world problems do not belong to single subjects. Future-ready curricula encourage learners to integrate perspectives from science, humanities, technology, and the arts.

The fourth principle is learner agency.

Students are active participants. They make choices, set goals, and reflect on their learning. Agency builds responsibility and motivation.

The fifth principle is ethical grounding.

What is important, is the learners to judge. As learners gain powerful tools, including AI, they must develop judgment. Curricula must address ethics, values, and social responsibility explicitly.

These principles do not replace academic rigor. They redefine it. Rigor becomes the ability to think, adapt, and act with integrity in unfamiliar situations.

Interdisciplinary ad project-based learning

Interdisciplinary and project-based learning translate future-ready principles into lived experience.

In traditional curricula, subjects are siloed. Knowledge is taught in isolation, and learners are rarely asked to connect ideas across domains. This limits transfer and relevance.

Project-based learning changes the structure of learning. Learners engage with complex, real-world problems that require multiple perspectives. They research, design, collaborate, and reflect over extended periods. Learning becomes contextual rather than abstract.

Interdisciplinary projects mirror how knowledge functions outside school. A single project may integrate science, mathematics, language, ethics, and technology. Learners learn not just content, but how disciplines interact.

Teachers act as facilitators and designers. They guide inquiry, ensure conceptual rigor, and help learners reflect on process and outcomes. Assessment focuses on understanding, problem-solving, and collaboration rather than isolated answers.

AI enhances project-based learning by providing access to data, simulations, and tools for analysis and creation. But projects must remain learner-driven. AI supports inquiry; it does not define it.

Without clear goals and reflection, projects risk becoming superficial. Depth comes from sustained inquiry and thoughtful scaffolding.

When done well, interdisciplinary and project-based learning prepare learners for complexity rather than certainty.

Creativity, critical thinking, and problem solving

In an AI-rich world, the value of human contribution shifts.

When machines can generate answers, the ability to ask meaningful questions becomes critical. Creativity, critical thinking, and problem-solving move from "soft skills" to core curriculum outcomes.

Creativity is not limited to artistic expression.

It includes imagining alternatives, reframing problems, and generating novel approaches. Future-ready curricula create space for experimentation and originality rather than penalizing deviation from expected answers.

Critical thinking involves evaluating information, recognizing bias, and constructing reasoned arguments. With AI-generated content becoming ubiquitous, discernment becomes essential.

Problem-solving requires learners to navigate ambiguity.

Problems are no longer well-defined exercises with single correct answers. They are complex, contextual, and evolving. Learners must analyze constraints, collaborate, test solutions, and adapt.

Curricula must therefore prioritize process over product. Learners should document thinking, reflect on decisions, and learn from failure. Assessment focuses on reasoning, not just outcomes.

Teachers play a key role in modeling these capabilities. They ask open-ended questions, challenge assumptions, and create environments where uncertainty is acceptable.

AI can support ideation and analysis, but it cannot replace human judgment.

The future belongs not to those who know the most, but to those who can think clearly, creatively, and ethically.

Ethical reasoning and values integration

As technology expands human capability, it also amplifies consequences.

Decisions made by individuals, especially when supported by AI, can affect communities, economies, and societies. A future-ready curriculum must therefore place ethical reasoning and values at its core.

Ethics cannot be treated as a separate subject taught in isolation.

Values must be integrated across disciplines and learning experiences. Learners should encounter ethical questions within science, technology, business, and social studies—not only in moral education classes.

This integration begins with contextual dilemmas. Students explore real-world scenarios involving data privacy, bias, environmental impact, and social responsibility. They learn to weigh competing interests and consider long-term effects. Teachers guide discussion rather than prescribe answers.

The goal is not moral conformity, but moral reasoning. Learners develop the ability to articulate values, listen to diverse perspectives, and justify decisions.

AI complicates ethical education. Students must understand authorship, responsibility, and accountability when using AI tools. They must learn when assistance becomes dependence and when efficiency compromises integrity.

Curricula should encourage reflection on why and how technology is used, not just whether it works.

Values-driven education anchors learning in humanity. It ensures that as learners gain power through knowledge and tools, they also gain wisdom.

Assessment-aligned curriculum

Curriculum reform fails when assessment remains unchanged.

No matter how flexible or future-focused a curriculum claims to be, learners will prioritize what is assessed. If assessments reward recall and speed, deeper learning remains peripheral.

A future-ready curriculum requires assessment to be aligned with its goals.

Assessment must evaluate understanding, application, and reasoning—not just content coverage. It should capture how learners think, collaborate, and adapt.

This demands a shift from isolated tests to authentic evidence of learning. Projects, portfolios, presentations, reflections, and problem-solving tasks become central. These formats allow learners to demonstrate competence in context.

Formative assessment plays a key role. Feedback is continuous and constructive. Learners receive guidance while learning is still unfolding, not only at the end.

AI can assist by capturing evidence, tracking progress, and offering feedback. But assessment decisions must remain transparent and interpretable.

- Over-automation risks reducing complex learning to simplified metrics.
- Teachers remain responsible for judgment, synthesis, and ethical oversight.
- When assessment aligns with curriculum intent, learning behaviors change naturally.
- Students invest in understanding because it is what counts.

Integrating AI into curriculum design

Integrating AI into curriculum design is not about adding a new subject. It is about rethinking how learning is structured, supported, and sustained.

When AI is treated as an external tool, it creates disruption. When it is embedded thoughtfully, it enhances coherence.

Curriculum design in the AI era begins with clarity of purpose. Leaders and educators must decide what learners should become, not just what they should know. AI then supports those aims rather than driving them.

AI can support curriculum design in several ways.

- It can help map competencies across subjects, identifying overlaps and progression.
- It can analyze learning data to reveal where curricula succeed or fall short.
- It can offer adaptive resources that respond to diverse learner needs.

However, curriculum authority must remain human.

AI can suggest content sequences, but it cannot judge cultural relevance, ethical alignment, or developmental appropriateness. These decisions require professional judgment and contextual understanding.

Teachers and curriculum designers must also address AI literacy. Learners should understand how AI works at a conceptual level: its strengths, limitations, and biases. This understanding empowers responsible use rather than passive dependence.

Curricula should make AI visible, not invisible. When learners are encouraged to question AI outputs, reflect on use, and consider consequences, they develop agency rather than reliance.

Integrated thoughtfully, AI strengthens curriculum responsiveness without eroding educational values.

Teacher role in curriculum transformation

Curriculum transformation happens in classroom, not on paper.

No matter how progressive a curriculum framework is, its success depends on how teachers interpret, adapt, and enact it. In the AI era, teachers are not just implementars but they are the active co-creators of the curriculum.

Traditional systems position teachers as followers of prescribed syllabi. Deviations are often discouraged in the name of consistency. This limits responsiveness and innovation.

Future-ready curricula require the opposite. Teachers must be trusted to:

- Adapt content to learner context
- Integrate interdisciplinary connections
- Modify pacing based on readiness
- Design meaningful learning experiences

Teachers can use AI-generated insights to refine sequencing, identify gaps, and personalize learning pathways, but transformation depends on teacher judgement, not automation.

Time for planning, collaboration, and reflection is essential. Professional learning communities enable shared experimentation and collective sense-making.

Leadership strategies for curriculum innovation

Curriculum innovation succeeds or fails at the leadership level. Teachers may experiment, learners may respond positively, and tools may be available, but without leadership alignment, innovation remains fragile and temporary.

Leaders must first provide permission to change.

In many systems, fear of deviation is deeply ingrained. Leaders must explicitly signal that adaptation, iteration, and even failure are part of responsible curriculum work. Without this psychological safety, innovation stays superficial.

Second, leaders must align policy with practice.

Assessment rules, reporting formats, timetables, and accountability structures must support future-ready learning. When innovative curricula are judged by outdated metrics, contradiction erodes momentum.

Third, leadership must invest in infrastructure and capability.

This includes technology access, teacher professional development, and collaborative planning time. Curriculum innovation cannot be sustained through individual effort alone.

Fourth, leaders must act as connectors.

They bridge classrooms with communities, industry, higher education, and global perspectives. These connections ensure curriculum relevance and expose learners to real-world complexity.

Finally, leaders must model learning.

When leadership demonstrates curiosity, reflection, and ethical use of AI, it sets cultural norms. Learners and teachers follow what leaders practice more than what they declare.

Reflection questions for leaders

A future-ready curriculum requires continuous reflection rather than fixed answers.

The following questions are designed to guide leaders as contexts, technologies, and learner needs evolve.

- Where does our current curriculum assume a predictable future?
- How well does our curriculum support transfer, adaptability, and ethical judgment?
- Which structures restrict flexibility and learner choice?
- How aligned are assessment practices with curriculum intent?
- In what ways are teachers empowered to adapt and co-create curriculum?
- How thoughtfully is AI integrated into curriculum design and delivery?
- What leadership behaviors must shift to sustain innovation over time?

Case Study: Reconfiguring India's Education for the AI Era

Source Material: National Education Policy (NEP) 2020

1. The Challenge: The "Knowledge Landscape" Shift

The NEP 2020 acknowledges that the world is undergoing rapid changes due to dramatic scientific and technological advances, specifically the rise of Big Data, Machine Learning, and Artificial AI.

- The Problem: Traditional education focused heavily on "factual and procedural knowledge," which computers can now handle better than humans.
- The Risk: Many unskilled jobs may be taken over by machines, making traditional "rote learning" and "learning-for-exams" obsolete for future employment.

2. The Curricular Intervention: "Learning How to Learn"

To remain competitive, the NEP proposes a total revision of the curriculum to emphasize higher-order cognitive capacities.

- New Subjects: AI, Design Thinking, and Data Science are introduced at relevant stages to ensure students are prepared for the "Fourth Industrial Revolution".
- Computational Thinking: Increased emphasis on mathematics and computational thinking will start from the Foundational Stage, using puzzles and games to make it engaging.
- Coding: Activities involving coding will be introduced as early as the Middle Stage (Grades 6-8).

- Reduced Content: To make room for AI-related critical thinking, the mandated curriculum content is being reduced in each subject to its "core essentials".

3. The Assessment Shift: From Summative to Formative

The policy realizes that if the test doesn't change, the teaching won't change. Therefore, it proposes a transformation in how students are evaluated:

- 360-Degree Progress Cards: Instead of a single "mark sheet," students will receive a holistic report reflecting progress in cognitive, affective, and psychomotor domains.
- AI-Based Tracking: The policy suggests developing AI-based software to track a student's growth over their entire school career, helping them identify strengths and make better career choices based on their learning data.
- Higher-Order Skills: National assessments (like those from the new center, PARAKH) will shift away from testing memorization and instead test "analysis, critical thinking, and conceptual clarity".

4. Teacher & Institutional Empowerment

- AI Research: Universities will offer Ph.D. and Master's programs in core areas like Machine Learning and multidisciplinary "AI + X" fields (e.g., AI + Healthcare, AI + Law).
- Digital Infrastructure: The National Educational Technology Forum (NETF) will be established to provide evidence-based advice on technology-based interventions and research in AI.

5. Key Takeaways (The NEP Vision)

The ultimate goal of this curriculum change is to bridge the gap between current learning outcomes and the requirements of the 21st century. By focusing on multidisciplinary abilities across sciences and humanities, India aims to transform into a "global knowledge superpower" that can lead in the AI-driven global ecosystem.

https://www.education.gov.in/sites/upload_files/mhrd/files/NEP_Final_English_0.pdf

CHAPTER 8

ASSESSMENT REIMAGINED—FROM JUDGEMENT TO GROWTH

Traditional assessment paradigm

For the longest time, assessment has been treated as the final act of learning. Students study, perform, and are judged on those basis. Marks are recorded, ranks are assigned, and learning moves on, often without any reflections. In this type of assessment, understanding is less.

This model emerged in a time when education systems needed efficiency and standardization. Large number of learners had to be evaluated quickly and comparably. Exams and grades served that purpose.

The benefits of the traditional system should not be underestimated. Standardized assessment provided structure and consistency. They offered clarity for institutions, parents, and employers. For many learners, it created motivation and a clear sense of expectation.

However, the limitations are now increasingly visible. Traditional assessment systems prioritize recall over reasoning. They reward speed rather than depth. They compress diverse abilities into single scores and often confuse performance with potential. Most importantly, they position assessment as judgement rather than support.

Failure becomes an endpoint instead of information. Feedback arrives too late to shape learning. Anxiety replaces curosity.

In an AI enabled world, where information is abundant and answers are accessible, this paradigm becomes even less relevant. What matters is not what learners can reproduce, but what they can understand, apply, and reflect upon.

Assessment must move from being a tool of control to a tool for growth.

From summative to formative assessment

Summative assessment tells us what happened.

Formative assessment helps shape what happens next.

Traditional systems rely heavily on summative assessments: end-of-term exams, final projects, standardized tests. These assessments record outcomes, but they arrive after learning opportunities have passed.

Formative assessment shifts the purpose of evaluation. Instead of asking *"How did the student perform?"*, it asks *"What does the student need now?"*

This approach treats assessment as an ongoing process embedded within learning. Feedback is timely, specific, and actionable. Learners adjust strategies while concepts are still forming.

The benefits are significant.

- Learners develop awareness of their own thinking.
- Mistakes become information, not failure.
- Teachers gain insight into misconceptions before they harden.

Formative assessment reduces anxiety as well. When progress is measured continuously, no single moment defines success or failure. Learning becomes iterative rather than high-stakes.

AI strengthens formative assessment when used responsibly. It provides instant feedback, identifies learning gaps, and tracks progress over time. But feedback alone is not formative. Interpretation and guidance matter as well.

Teachers decide how feedback is framed, when to intervene, and how to support emotional response. Human judgment remains central.

Importantly, formative assessment does not replace summative assessment entirely.

Summative assessments still serve accountability and certification purposes. The shift is about balance, not elimination.

When formative assessment leads and summative assessment follows, learning improves naturally.

Assessment becomes a companion to learning, not its conclusion.

Competency-based assessment

Marks tell us how a learner performed at a moment in time. Competencies tell us what a learner can actually do.

Competency-based assessment shifts focus from scores to demonstrated abilities. Learners progress by mastering clearly defined skills and understandings rather than by accumulating marks or seat time. This approach aligns naturally with personalized and future-ready education.

Competencies are transparent. Learners know what they are working toward and what mastery looks like. Progress becomes visible and meaningful. Competency-based systems also allow flexibility. Learners move at different paces. They revisit concepts without stigma. Time becomes a resource, not a constraint.

Assessment focuses on evidence. Projects, performances, simulations, and portfolios show how learners apply knowledge in context. Mastery is demonstrated through action, not recall.

AI supports competency-based assessment by tracking evidence across time and contexts. It helps map progress and identify gaps.

However, defining competencies requires care. Overly narrow competencies fragment learning. Overly broad ones lack clarity. Teachers and leaders must collaborate to define meaningful, integrated competencies.

Authentic assessment

Authentic assessment asks learners to use knowledge the way it is used outside school.

Instead of answering questions detached from context, learners engage in tasks that mirror real-world challenges. They analyze, create, collaborate, and justify decisions. This approach bridges the gap between learning and application. Examples include designing solutions, conducting investigations, presenting proposals, or reflecting on real scenarios. These tasks demand understanding, not memorization.

Authentic assessment supports deeper learning. Learners must integrate multiple skills—critical thinking, communication, ethical reasoning and collaboration. They learn to manage ambiguity rather than search for predefined answers.

Teachers play a crucial role in designing authentic assessments. Tasks must be meaningful, aligned with competencies, and appropriately challenging. Clear criteria ensures rigor and fairness.

AI enhances authenticity when used responsibly. It can simulate environments, provide data sets, and support analysis. But learners must remain accountable for decisions and reasoning.

Assessment becomes a learning experience in itself. When learners see relevance, motivation increases. Assessment stops being a hurdle and becomes an opportunity to demonstrate growth.

Assessment and AI integration

AI is reshaping assessment faster than any reform in recent history. It can generate questions, analyze responses, provide instant feedback, and track learning patterns. Used thoughtfully, it reduces administrative load and supports timely intervention. Used carelessly, it risks reducing learning to metrics.

The purpose of AI in assessment must be clear. AI should support insight, not replace judgment. It identifies trends and signals, but educators interpret meaning and decide action.

AI works best in formative contexts. It can offer immediate feedback on practice tasks, highlight misconceptions, and suggest resources. This accelerates learning cycles without raising stakes.

In summative contexts, caution is essential. Automated grading may work for objective responses, but complex reasoning, creativity, and ethical judgment resist automation. Overreliance on AI scoring risks flattening learning.

Transparency is non-negotiable. Learners must know when AI is used, how decisions are made, and how to challenge outcomes. Trust depends on clarity.

Ethical considerations extend beyond accuracy. Data privacy, bias, and fairness must be addressed proactively. AI systems reflect the assumptions embedded in their design.

Ultimately, assessment remains a human responsibility. AI extends capacity, but accountability remains with educators.

Self and peer assessment

When learners participate in assessment, learning deepens.

Self and peer assessment shift responsibility from teacher-only judgment to shared reflection. Learners learn to evaluate quality, recognize progress, and identify areas for improvement.

Self-assessment builds metacognition.

Learners reflect on their thinking, strategies, and outcomes. They learn to ask: *What did I understand? What challenged me? What will I do differently next time?* This awareness strengthens independence and lifelong learning habits.

Peer assessment develops perspective and communication. By reviewing others' work, learners sharpen their own understanding of standards. They practice giving constructive feedback and receiving critique, skills essential beyond school.

Clear criteria are essential. Self and peer assessment succeed when expectations are transparent and guidance is provided. Without structure, feedback becomes vague or personal.

AI can support these practices by organizing evidence, prompting reflection, and managing workflows. But reflection itself must remain human.

Teachers guide the process. They model feedback, ensure psychological safety, and intervene when misunderstandings arise. When learners are trusted as assessors, assessment becomes a learning tool, not a verdict.

Leadership in assessment transformation

Assessment reform does not succeed through classroom innovation alone.

Leaders determine whether new assessment practices are protected, scaled, or quietly abandoned. Without leadership alignment, teachers face conflicting expectations.

The first leadership responsibility is intent clarity.

Leaders must clearly articulate why assessment is being reimagined and how it supports learning goals. Without this clarity, change is perceived as added complexity rather than meaningful improvement.

Second, leaders must align policies and accountability.

Reporting systems, external examinations, and performance metrics must reflect growth-oriented assessment. When innovative assessment is judged by outdated standards, tension undermines progress.

Third, leadership must invest in teacher capacity.

Assessment literacy is essential. Teachers need support in designing tasks, developing criteria, and interpreting evidence. Professional development must go beyond tool training to include judgment and ethics.

Fourth, leaders must protect professional trust.

Teachers need autonomy to assess holistically. Over-standardization undermines the aspects of growth assessment, the very idea that it seeks to support.

Finally, leaders must communicate with stakeholders.

Parents, learners, and institutions must understand new assessment approaches. Transparency builds confidence and reduces resistance.

Ethical considerations in AI enabled assessment

When AI enters assessment, ethics move from the margins to the center.

Assessment decisions shape confidence, opportunity, and future pathways. Any system that influences these outcomes must be held to the highest ethical standards.

The first concern is fairness.

AI systems are trained on data. If that data reflects historical bias, the system can reproduce or amplify inequity. Learners from certain backgrounds may be unfairly advantaged or penalized unless safeguards are in place.

The second concern is transparency.

Learners and educators must understand how assessment decisions are made. Black-box systems undermine trust and remove agency. Any AI-supported assessment must be explainable and open to review.

The third concern is privacy and data protection.

Assessment data is deeply personal. Clear policies are required around data collection, storage, access, and retention. Learners should know what data is collected and how it is used.

The fourth concern is over-automation.

When AI takes on too much authority, human judgment weakens. Ethical assessment requires teachers to retain final responsibility for interpretation and decisions.

Ethical use of AI must be taught, not assumed. Learners should engage with discussions about bias, authorship, and responsibility. Assessment becomes an opportunity to build ethical awareness, not just measure performance. Ethics are not constraints on innovation. They are what make innovation trustworthy.

Linking assessment to lifelong learning

Assessment shapes how learners view learning long after formal education ends. When assessment is experienced as judgment, learners associate learning with fear, compliance, or external validation. When assessment supports growth, learners develop habits that extend into adulthood.

Lifelong learning depends on self-awareness and adaptability. Learners must be able to evaluate their own skills, identify gaps, and seek improvement without external prompts. Growth-oriented assessment builds these capabilities early.

Competency-based and formative approaches help learners track progress over time. They learn to reflect on feedback, set goals, and adjust strategies—skills essential in changing professional landscapes.

Assessment also becomes less episodic. Instead of isolated exams, learning evidence accumulates. Portfolios, reflections, and projects create a narrative of growth rather than snapshots of performance.

AI can support lifelong learning by helping learners visualize progress and identify future learning needs. But motivation remains human. Learners must see assessment as a tool they can use, not something done to them. When assessment fosters agency, learners remain curious, reflective, and open to growth throughout life.

Framework—assessment for growth

To move from intent to practice, schools need a clear framework that aligns assessment with learning, equity, and ethics.

An Assessment for Growth framework rests on five core principles.

1. Purpose Over Performance

Assessment exists to support learning, not merely record results. Every assessment should inform next steps for learners and teachers.

2. Evidence Over Scores

Learning is demonstrated through authentic evidence—projects, portfolios, reflections—not reduced to single numbers.

3. Progress Over Comparison

Learners are evaluated against competencies and personal growth, not against peers.

4. Human Judgment Over Automation

AI supports insight and efficiency, but educators retain responsibility for interpretation and decisions.

5. Transparency and Trust

Learners understand criteria, processes, and outcomes. Assessment decisions are explainable and open to dialogue.

Reflection questions for leaders

Assessment reform requires ongoing reflection rather than fixed solutions.

- What purposes does assessment currently serve in our system?
- How aligned are assessment practices with learning goals?
- Where does over-standardization restrict growth?
- How responsibly is AI used in assessment?
- How well do learners understand and trust assessment processes?

- What leadership actions are needed to sustain growth-oriented assessment?

Case Study: Leveraging Generative AI for Iterative Course Design

Institution: Harvard Kennedy School (HKS) Lead Researcher: Dan Levy, Senior Lecturer in Public Policy

1. The Challenge: The "Noise" of Feedback

At the end of every semester, instructors receive a high volume of qualitative student evaluations. Levy identified three primary hurdles that prevent this feedback from improving education:

- The Extremity Bias: Teachers tend to remember the "glowing" praise or the "harsh" criticism, ignoring the average experience of the majority.
- The Time Gap: Evaluations are read months before the course is taught again, causing specific actionable details to be forgotten.
- Data Overload: In large classes, manually coding 100+ open-ended comments to find recurring themes is time-prohibitive.

2. The Intervention: The TIC Framework

Levy implemented a workflow using Generative AI (specifically LLMs like ChatGPT) to act as a Pedagogical Analyst. He developed the TIC (Task, Instructions, Context) formula to ensure the AI's suggestions were grounded in the actual course structure.

3. The Implementation Process

The process followed a three-step cycle:

- Data Integration: Anonymized student evaluations and the official course syllabus were uploaded to the AI.
- Thematic Distillation: The AI was tasked with identifying exactly three strengths and three weaknesses based on student consensus, not outliers.
- Actionable Translation: The instructor asked the AI for "realistic, low-friction changes" that could be made to the syllabus to address the weaknesses.

4. Findings & Results

By using AI to analyze his own "Quantitative Methods" course at Harvard, Levy discovered several key insights that had previously been buried in the text:

- Identified Weakness: Students felt a "time pressure" during technical weeks (e.g., Monte Carlo simulations).
- AI-Generated Solution: The AI suggested adding Visual Workload Markers to the syllabus.
- Outcome: Levy added asterisks to high-effort weeks, allowing students to plan their schedules better. This transparency directly addressed the "Pace and Depth" anxiety identified in previous evaluations.

5. Key Takeaways for Educators

The Harvard study concludes that AI serves as a bridge between Information and Action.

1. Efficiency: AI can distill a semester's worth of feedback into a 2-minute summary.

2. Objectivity: It removes the emotional sting of reading harsh reviews by focusing on logical patterns.
3. Scaffolding: It allows for "Mid-course corrections" (using AI to analyze discussion boards) rather than waiting for the end of the year.

Conclusion

This case study proves that AI's greatest value in education may not be in "replacing" the teacher, but in empowering the teacher to listen better to their students.

https://hbsp.harvard.edu/inspiring-minds/ai-course-evaluations-better-teaching

CHAPTER 9

EQUITY, ACCESS, AND INCLUSION IN THE AI ERA

The Imperative for Equity in Education

Equity has always been central to the promise of education. Schools exist not only to transmit knowledge, but to expand opportunity. Yet despite decades of reform, educational outcomes remain deeply unequal. Technology, including AI, has the potential to narrow or widen these gaps.

Equity is not the same as equality. Equality provides the same resources to everyone. Equity provides what each learner needs to succeed. In diverse classrooms, uniform approaches often reinforce disadvantage rather than reduce it.

Access to devices, connectivity, digital literacy, and supportive environments varies widely. Without deliberate design, AI-enhanced education risks benefiting those who already have advantage.

Equity must therefore be a foundational principle, not a downstream concern. This requires confronting uncomfortable truths about systemic bias, resource allocation, and institutional practices. It also requires moving beyond symbolic inclusion toward structural change.

AI can be a powerful lever for equity when used responsibly.

It can personalize learning, support accessibility, and identify learners who need additional support. But tools alone cannot solve inequity.

Human values, leadership choices, and policy decisions determine outcomes.

Equity in the AI era is not automatic. It is intentional work.

Understanding the dimensions of inclusion

Inclusion in the AI era cannot be reduced to a simple question of access. It is not only about who has a device or who can log into a platform. Inclusion is about whether every learner—regardless of background, language, ability, or circumstance—can meaningfully participate, progress, and feel seen within the system. AI has the power to strengthen this participation. It also has the power to quietly restrict it. The difference lies in how we design, distribute, and supervise these systems.

From an economic perspective, AI offers unprecedented opportunity. High-quality learning materials, tutoring support, and adaptive practice systems can reach students who previously had limited academic guidance. A learner in a remote town can now receive explanations, practice feedback, and exposure to global knowledge that once required proximity to elite institutions. In this sense, AI can act as a bridge.

Geography presents a similar dual reality. AI-powered education can transcend physical boundaries. It can bring specialized instruction to underserved regions and connect learners across distances. However, many AI systems assume reliable connectivity, uninterrupted electricity, and individual device ownership. For students navigating unstable infrastructure, these assumptions turn innovation into frustration. Inclusion, therefore, requires more than deployment; it demands design that accounts for constraints rather than ignoring them.

Language and culture form another crucial dimension. AI systems increasingly support translation, multilingual interfaces, and localized content. This creates possibilities for students to learn in languages they are comfortable with, reducing barriers that traditional systems often imposed. At the same time, much of the underlying training data for AI models reflects dominant global languages and perspectives. Subtle cultural biases can shape examples, assessments, and even definitions of success. If learners constantly encounter unfamiliar contexts, their engagement may diminish. True inclusion means ensuring that AI does not standardize AI around a single cultural lens.

When it comes to cognitive diversity, AI offers remarkable promise. Adaptive systems can adjust pace, provide additional practice where needed, and reduce the stigma often attached to struggling in public. Students who require more time or different forms of explanation can receive tailored support. This personalization can strengthen confidence and autonomy.

However, personalization carries risk when it turns into prediction. If algorithms begin to categorize students too early—identifying them as "high potential" or "at risk"—they may unintentionally narrow opportunities. Labels, even when generated by machines, can influence expectations and outcomes. Inclusion requires that AI remain flexible, allowing learners to grow beyond past performance rather than being confined by it.

For learners with disabilities, AI can be transformative. Speech recognition, text-to-speech, real-time captioning, and alternative input systems expand participation in ways traditional classrooms struggled to accommodate. These tools can promote independence and dignity. Yet inclusion weakens when accessibility is treated as an optional enhancement rather than a standard design principle. Systems built without universal design in mind often exclude by default, requiring retroactive adjustments that never fully close the gap.

There is also a dimension of inclusion that technology struggles to quantify: emotional and psychological belonging. AI can optimize content delivery, track performance patterns, and generate recommendations, but it cannot replace the relational trust between teacher and student. A learner who feels invisible or misunderstood may disengage regardless of technological sophistication. In this respect, inclusion depends not only on tools, but on human connection guiding their use.

Understanding the dimensions of inclusion in the AI era means accepting this tension. AI is neither inherently equitable nor inherently exclusionary. It amplifies the values embedded within it. When designed thoughtfully, it can extend opportunity, personalize learning, and reduce long-standing barriers. When implemented carelessly, it can reinforce hierarchy, bias, and imbalance.

The responsibility, therefore, does not rest with the technology alone. It rests with educators, leaders, policymakers, and designers who decide how AI will function within educational systems. Inclusion in the AI age is not achieved by simply providing access. It is achieved by ensuring that every learner has not only the tools, but the support, dignity, and opportunity to use them fully.

Equity through Curriculum and Pedagogy

Equity in education is shaped not only by who enters the classroom, but by what is taught and how learning unfolds. Curriculum and pedagogy determine whether students see themselves reflected in knowledge and whether they are given fair opportunities to succeed. In the AI era, these dimensions hold renewed promise. When thoughtfully designed, technology can strengthen equity by expanding representation, personalizing instruction, and empowering learners to grow at their own pace.

An equitable curriculum ensures that knowledge is not limited to a single perspective. AI-supported systems make it possible to integrate diverse voices, regional histories, and interdisciplinary viewpoints more seamlessly than ever before. Digital platforms can curate materials from across cultures and contexts, allowing students to encounter a broader intellectual landscape. Learners are no longer confined to a fixed textbook; they can access evolving, relevant content that reflects both global developments and local realities. This expanded access nurtures intellectual inclusion and validates multiple ways of understanding the world.

Traditional instruction often required teachers to move at a uniform pace, leaving some students overwhelmed and others unchallenged. Adaptive technologies now allow lessons to respond dynamically to individual progress. Students can revisit concepts, receive targeted explanations, and practice until they achieve confidence. This responsiveness reduces comparison and creates space for mastery without stigma. Each learner is supported according to their needs rather than measured against a single benchmark.

AI also strengthens formative feedback, making assessment more continuous and constructive. Instead of waiting for periodic exams, students can receive real-time insights into their progress. This encourages reflection and active engagement with learning. As students monitor their development, they cultivate self-awareness and responsibility. Equity grows when learners are given tools that help them understand their strengths and areas for improvement without fear or embarrassment.

Another powerful dimension of equity lies in learner agency. AI tools can support inquiry-based projects, simulations, and creative problem-solving. Students can experiment with ideas, test hypotheses, and refine their work with guided assistance. This expands access to high-quality mentorship and intellectual support that was once limited by classroom ratios.

Teachers remain central to this transformation. With AI handling routine tasks and providing data-driven insights, educators gain more time to focus on mentorship, discussion, and individualized guidance. This strengthens relationships within the classroom and allows instruction to be more responsive and inclusive. Technology becomes a support system that amplifies the teacher's capacity to reach every student.

When curriculum reflects diverse perspectives and pedagogy adapts to individual growth, education moves closer to equity. AI, when aligned with thoughtful design and professional expertise, can help create classrooms where every learner has the opportunity to participate fully, progress meaningfully, and see their potential recognized.

Closing the digital divide

Closing the digital divide is central to building an inclusive education system in the AI era. Access to technology is no longer a supplementary advantage; it shapes how learners engage with knowledge, develop skills, and participate in modern society. Bridging this divide is not simply about distributing devices, it is about ensuring meaningful, sustained, and confident use of digital tools.

Infrastructure forms the foundation. Reliable connectivity, functional devices, and stable digital platforms create the conditions for participation. When schools and communities are equipped with dependable technological resources, learners can access adaptive learning systems, digital libraries, collaborative tools, and AI-supported feedback without interruption. Investment in public digital infrastructure strengthens educational continuity and reduces disparities between regions.

Beyond infrastructure, digital literacy plays an equally important role. Learners must understand how to navigate platforms, evaluate information, and use AI tools responsibly. Closing the divide involves equipping students with the confidence to interact critically with technology rather than passively consuming it. When learners are taught how digital systems function, they become informed participants rather than dependent users. This shift from access to capability transforms technology into a genuine equalizer.

Teachers are central to this transition. Professional development in digital and AI literacy enables educators to integrate tools effectively into pedagogy. When teachers feel confident guiding students through digital environments, classrooms become more dynamic and inclusive. Support structures for educators ensure that technology enhances instruction rather than becoming an additional burden.

Community involvement further strengthens efforts to close the divide. Partnerships between schools, local institutions, and policymakers can expand access points and provide shared learning spaces. Libraries, community centers, and public initiatives can extend connectivity and resources beyond school hours, ensuring that learning continues beyond classroom walls.

AI itself can contribute to narrowing gaps by offering scalable support. Intelligent tutoring systems and multilingual interfaces provide academic assistance across distances. Offline-compatible platforms and low-bandwidth solutions make digital learning more resilient in varied contexts. Thoughtful design ensures that innovation reaches learners in diverse environments rather than concentrating in already advantaged spaces.

Closing the digital divide ultimately means ensuring that technology serves as a bridge rather than a boundary. When infrastructure, literacy, teacher preparation, and community engagement align, digital tools become instruments of participation and progress. In such an ecosystem, AI does not create hierarchy; it expands opportunity, enabling learners from all backgrounds to engage confidently in a connected world.

Inclusive Assessment Practices

Assessment shapes not only academic outcomes but also learners' confidence, motivation, and sense of belonging. When assessment practices are inclusive, they create opportunities for every learner to demonstrate understanding in ways that reflect their strengths. In the AI era, assessment can move beyond narrow measurement toward a more responsive and supportive model of growth.

Inclusive assessment recognizes that learners express knowledge differently. Some communicate effectively through writing, others through projects, presentations, design, or practical application. Digital platforms and AI-supported tools allow for varied formats of evidence. Students can build portfolios, document progress through multimedia reflections, and demonstrate mastery through simulations or collaborative tasks. This flexibility ensures that achievement is not limited to a single mode of performance.

Formative feedback becomes more continuous and accessible with AI integration. Instead of relying solely on high-stakes exams, learners can receive timely insights into their progress. Immediate feedback supports correction, refinement, and deeper understanding. When students are encouraged to revise and improve rather than simply accept a grade, assessment becomes part of the learning process rather than a conclusion to it.

Personalization also strengthens inclusivity. Adaptive systems can adjust the level of challenge, provide additional support where needed, and identify patterns in performance that help educators respond thoughtfully. This responsiveness reduces the pressure of comparison and allows learners to focus on progress. Students who require more time or alternative explanations can move forward with confidence.

Transparency plays a vital role in inclusive assessment. Learners benefit when evaluation criteria are clear and when they understand how feedback is generated. AI tools can visualize progress, helping students track growth over time. When assessment systems are understandable and open, they build trust and encourage active engagement.

Inclusive assessment also supports self-reflection. Digital tools can prompt learners to set goals, review their work, and identify areas for improvement. Over time, this fosters self-awareness and responsibility. Students begin to view evaluation not as external judgment, but as a resource for development. Such habits extend beyond formal education and strengthen lifelong learning.

Teachers remain central in guiding inclusive assessment practices. AI can provide data and analytics, but educators interpret context, recognize effort, and respond with empathy. Their professional judgment ensures that technology supports fairness rather than replacing human insight.

When assessment practices are flexible, transparent, and growth-oriented, they reinforce dignity and confidence. In the AI-supported classroom, inclusive assessment becomes a mechanism for empowerment. It validates diverse abilities, supports steady improvement, and ensures that every learner has the opportunity to demonstrate understanding in meaningful ways.

Teacher Role in Equity and Inclusion

Equity and inclusion in education are ultimately sustained by the people who stand at the center of the classroom. While AI can expand access, personalize instruction, and generate insights, it is the teacher who translates these possibilities into meaningful practice. Technology can support inclusion, but teachers give it direction, intention, and humanity.

Teachers shape classroom culture. They establish whether differences are treated as deficits or as strengths. In inclusive environments, diversity of thought, pace, language, and background is acknowledged openly and respected. AI tools may provide data about learning patterns, but it is the teacher who interprets those patterns within the broader context of a student's life. This interpretive role is critical for equity. Numbers and dashboards offer signals; educators provide understanding.

In AI-supported classrooms, teachers act as guides rather than gatekeepers. With access to adaptive platforms and real-time feedback systems, they can identify where learners need additional support or greater challenge. This enables more responsive instruction. Students who might once have been overlooked in large, uniform systems can receive timely attention. Technology highlights needs, but teachers respond with judgment, empathy, and encouragement.

Equity also depends on how teachers frame the use of AI itself. When educators model critical thinking about digital tools, questioning outputs, discussing limitations, and emphasizing ethical use, students learn to engage thoughtfully rather than passively. This strengthens inclusion by ensuring that all learners develop confidence in navigating AI, regardless of their background. Teachers help students move from simply using technology to understanding and shaping it.

Professional growth plays a role as well. When teachers are supported in developing digital and AI literacy, they are better equipped to design inclusive learning experiences. Ongoing training enables educators to integrate tools in ways that enhance participation rather than complicate it. Empowered teachers create empowered classrooms.

Perhaps most importantly, teachers cultivate belonging. AI systems can recommend resources and track performance, but they cannot replace the reassurance of a mentor who recognizes effort, notices struggle, and affirms potential. Inclusion is sustained through relationships. Students are more likely to engage deeply when they feel seen and valued.

In the AI era, the teacher's role evolves but does not diminish. Educators become orchestrators of human and technological collaboration, ensuring that innovation aligns with fairness and dignity. Equity flourishes not through automation alone, but through teachers who use every available tool to create classrooms where every learner has the opportunity to participate, grow, and succeed.

Leadership Strategies for Equity

Equity in the AI era does not emerge by chance. It reflects deliberate choices made by leaders who shape policy, allocate resources, and define institutional priorities. School heads, administrators, and policymakers influence whether technology becomes a tool for broad participation or a layer that benefits only a few. Leadership, therefore, plays a decisive role in translating the promise of AI into inclusive educational practice.

A strong equity strategy begins with vision. Leaders must articulate clearly that inclusion is not an auxiliary goal but a core principle guiding technology adoption. When equity is embedded in strategic planning, decisions about procurement, curriculum integration, and professional development are aligned with fairness from the outset. AI initiatives become part of a larger commitment to widening opportunity rather than isolated experiments in innovation.

Resource allocation is another critical dimension. Ensuring that infrastructure, connectivity, and devices are distributed equitably which requires intentional planning. Leaders who prioritize underserved schools and communities help create balanced ecosystems where digital access is not determined by geography or income. Investments in shared digital infrastructure, open platforms, and scalable solutions reinforce this commitment.

Professional development also reflects leadership priorities. Equipping teachers with digital and AI literacy strengthens their capacity to design inclusive classrooms. When educators are supported through training, collaboration, and ongoing guidance, technology integration becomes thoughtful and purposeful. Leaders who cultivate learning cultures among staff model the very adaptability they seek to nurture in students.

Ethical oversight forms an essential component of leadership strategy. Transparent guidelines around data privacy, algorithmic use, and student protection build trust within educational communities. Clear governance frameworks ensure that AI systems operate within defined boundaries that respect dignity and accountability. Leaders who establish review mechanisms and encourage dialogue around technology foster environments where innovation and responsibility coexist.

Collaboration strengthens equity efforts. Engaging parents, community stakeholders, and students in conversations about AI integration broadens perspective and enhances trust. Inclusive decision-making processes ensure that policies reflect diverse needs and lived realities. When communities feel heard, implementation becomes more grounded and sustainable.

Finally, leadership for equity requires continuous reflection. As technology evolves, so too must institutional strategies. Regular evaluation of outcomes, open channels for feedback, and willingness to adjust policies keep equity efforts responsive rather than static. Leaders who approach AI with both ambition and attentiveness create systems that adapt without losing sight of fairness.

In the AI-driven education landscape, leadership is not simply administrative oversight. It is stewardship. By aligning vision, resources, training, governance, and community engagement around inclusive goals, leaders ensure that innovation expands opportunity and strengthens participation for every learner.

Reflection Questions for Leaders

- Does our AI integration strengthen equity across curriculum, pedagogy, and assessment?
- Are we ensuring that AI tools are accessible across socioeconomic and geographic contexts?
- Do our systems support multilingual, culturally responsive learning experiences?
- Are teachers adequately prepared to use AI in ways that enhance inclusion?

CHAPTER 10

SCHOOLS AS VALUE-DRIVEN LEARNING ECOSYSTEMS – ANCHORING HUMANITY IN AN AI WORLD

The case for values in education

AI has become increasingly embedded in education, the conversation often centres on efficiency, personalization, and performance. Yet there is one question: What is education ultimately for? If schools become spaces optimized only for speed, output, and measurable outcomes, they risk losing the qualities that make learning meaningful. In an AI-drvien world, values are not an optional addition to education, they are its anchor.

Values guide how technology is used. Two schools may adopt the same AI, yet their outcomes will differ depending on the principles that shape implementation. In a value driven ecosystem, AI becomes a support for collaboration, critical thinking, and growth. Without clear ethical grounding, it may reinforce competition, surveiliance, or narrow definitions of success. Values determine whether technology enhances humanity or diminishes it.

Students must evaluate information authenticity, question algorithmic outputs, and consider the societal implications of emerging technologies since they are living in an AI-driven generation. Education that prioritizes values equips learners with the moral compass required to make responsible decisions. This helps shape the future thoughtfully as well.

Schools that emphasize respect, inclusion, and shared responsibility create environments where learners feel safe to question, experiment, and grow. This emotional securtiy strengthens engagement.

Anchoring education in values does not mean resisting innovation. It means guiding innovation with intention. In an AI world, defining advantage of schools will not be their technological sophistication alone, but their commitment to nurturing character alongside competence. When values shape learning ecosystems, technology serves human development rather than replacing it.

As machines become more capable, the distinctly human capabilities of empathy, ethical reasoning, collaboration, and reflective judgment become more vital. Schools that remain grounded in these principles will prepare learners to succeed in an AI-driven future as well as lead it responsibly.

Defining a value driven learning ecosystem

A value driven learning ecosystem is defined by its infrastructure, its rankings, or the sophistication of its technology as well as the principles that shape everyday decisions within it. In the AI world, where tools can optimize processes and automate functions, the distinguishing feature of a school is no longer efficiency alone; it is intention. A value driven ecosystem places human dignity, integrity, inclusion, and responsibility at the center of learning.

Such an ecosystem recognizes that education is relational before it is technological. Policies, curriculum choices, assessment practices, and AI integrations are guided by shared beliefs about what it means to grow as a person. Technology becomes a means, not an end. AI tools are evaluated not only for performance outcomes but for their alignment with fairness, transparency, and student well-being.

In a value driven environment, inclusion is woven into the fabric of learning. Diversity of thought, culture, language, and ability is respected and reflected in both content and pedagogy. Learners are encouraged to question, to reflect, and to engage ethically with digital systems. AI supports personalization and access, but it operates within clearly articulated boundaries that protect privacy and promote agency.

This ecosystem also nurtures character alongside competence. Students are guided to develop empathy, accountability and discernment as they interact with AI tools and digital information. They learn how to generate answers, and also to evaluate them.

Leadership and teacher practice reinforce these values consistently. Decisions about technology adoption, assessment design and resource allocation are anchored in shared principles rather than short-term trends. Professional development supports educators in integrating AI thoughtfully while maintaining relational depth within classrooms.

A value-driven learning ecosystem is dynamic rather than rigid. It adapts to technological change without losing sight of its core commitments. Feedback loops involving students, teachers, and communities ensure that practices remain aligned with institutional values.

In an AI world, where automation can accelerate learning processes, the defining strength of a school lies in the clarity of its moral compass. A values-driven ecosystem ensures that innovation strengthens humanity rather than overshadowing it. It prepares learners not only to function within advanced systems, but to lead with integrity in shaping them.

Embedding Ethics and Purpose in Curriculum

In today's times, knowledge alone is no longer sufficient. Information is abundant, answers are instant, and content is continuously generated. What distinguishes meaningful education is not the quantity of knowledge delivered, but the ethical and purposeful framework within which it is understood. Including ethics and purpose in the curriculum ensures that learning is guided by responsibility, reflection, and long-term thinking.

Ethics should not appear as a standalone module taught once. It has to be woven across disciplines. In science and technology, students can examine the societal implications of innovation. In social sciences, they can analyze how algorithms influence public opinion and access to opportunity. In literature and the arts, they can explore themes of identity, power, and human agency in a digital age. When ethical inquiry becomes interdisciplinary, learners begin to see its relevance in every domain.

Students are more likely to invest effort when they understand why their learning matters beyond examinations. Curriculum that connects academic content to real world challenges like sustainability, equity, digital citizenship, community well being, etc., learners situate their knowledge within broader contexts. AI tools can support this by enabling research, simulation, and global collaboration.

As students use AI-generated outputs, they must learn to question accuracy, bias, and intent. Classroom discussions can model how to evaluate digital information critically rather than accepting it passively. This habit of inquiry strengthens intellectual independence and prevents overreliance on automated systems.

Opportunities for journaling, dialogue, and project-based learning allow students to connect personal values with academic pursuits. They begin to view education not merely as preparation for employment, but as preparation for thoughtful participation in society. AI can enhance these by providing feedback and supporting exploration.

When ethics and purpose are embedded intentionally, curriculum moves beyond content delivery. It becomes a framework for shaping judgment, empathy, and responsibility. In an era where technological capacity is accelerating, education must ensure that moral reasoning grows alongside it. Schools that align knowledge with values prepare learners not only to navigate complex systems, but to influence them with integrity and intention.

Socio-Emotional Learning and Well-Being

As computers and machines are used more in schools, the things that make us human are even more important when we learn. Being good at school work is not enough to help us grow. Students need to know themselves be able to control their feelings care about others and deal with times. Learning about how to get along with people and understand our emotions helps students develop qualities that computers cannot teach. That are necessary, for doing well in a world that is changing because of artificial AI. Artificial AI is changing our world and socio-emotional learning is important for students to succeed in this AI world.

AI systems can make things personal. Keep track of how people do but they do not feel unsure get frustrated or doubt themselves. Students do feel these things.

Classrooms that focus on how students feel and get along with others know that learning is not about being smart. It is also about feeling good about yourself feeling like you are part of the group and wanting to learn.

When students feel safe and respected they are more willing to think about things and learn about new technologies, like artificial AI systems. Artificial AI systems are a part of these technologies.

In a school where people care about what's right the teachers also focus on teaching the students how to get along with others and understand their feelings. The students learn by talking to each other working together thinking about what they did and getting help, from someone who can guide them. This helps the students learn how to understand others and talk to people in a way. These are skills for the students to have especially when they grow up and have jobs because computers and machines are doing more and more work. Socio-emotional learning is a part of this and it helps the students become better people. The students learn socio- learning every day and it really helps them.

Well-being is really important. It also requires balance. When we use tools to get more information and to be more productive schools need to teach students how to use technology in a healthy way. This means students should know when to stop using technology they should think carefully about how they use it. They should remember that talking to people face to face is important. Technology, like AI can help us get things done faster but it should not replace the time we spend with people or the time we rest. Well-being and technology need to be balanced so that technology does not hurt our well-being.

Teachers are really important when it comes to showing students how to deal with their emotions. The way Teachers handle problems and difficult situations shows students how to stay calm and be respectful. Computers and machines can help us understand how students learn. They cannot give students the support and kindness that Teachers can. Teachers give students the confidence they need to keep going.

Learning about feelings and getting along with others helps people adapt to things. We live in a world where technology is always changing. It is really important to be able to deal with that and be open to learning new things. Students who know what they are good at can handle problems in a way and work well with others are better able to handle things when they are not sure what will happen. Socio-emotional learning is very important for students to learn how to be resilient and open, to growth and socio-emotional learning helps students learn how to collaborate and manage setbacks.

By embedding well-being into the fabric of schooling, educational institutions ensure that technological progress does not outpace human development. Socio-emotional learning keeps education grounded in empathy and balance, preparing learners not only to work alongside AI, but to remain centered and connected in its presence.

Teacher as Value Mentor

In a classroom where computers and machines help us learn we can find a lot of information. Get help right away. But what is really hard to find. Is someone to guide us on what's right and wrong. The teacher is not someone who teaches us things they are also someone who helps us figure out how to use the things we learn how to use computers and machines and how to treat other people. Teachers help us learn about things like being honest and caring about others. They teach us to be responsible, for what we do.

Students see a lot more than what they're actually taught in class. They pay attention to how their teachers react when people disagree with them. They notice how their teachers give feedback and how they handle mistakes. They also see how their teachers use tools.

In their interactions with teachers students learn what is important. When teachers are fair, respectful and make decisions students learn to do the same. Teachers show students how to use the information they get from things like AI in a smart way. Students learn from teachers not, from artificial AI because teachers show them how to apply what they know.

In classrooms where AI tools are used the teacher helps students use them in a way. The teacher talks to students about what AI tools can and cannot do. They want students to think carefully about the answers they get from AI tools. The teacher also makes sure students understand they are responsible for their school work. Students learn that AI tools are a tool to help them they still have to put in effort and think for themselves. Teachers have conversations, with students. Help them think about how to use AI tools in a way that is right and fair.

Teachers are like mentors. They help students understand that learning is not about being the best. It is about being ready to make a difference. When teachers talk to students about what they want to achieve how they can make an impact and how they can become people it helps students see that education is a part of being human. Computers can help students learn. Teachers are the ones who help students see how what they learn fits into their own life and into the world, around them. Teachers help students understand what is really important.

The mentoring role really helps students feel like they belong to the system. When students feel like someone is paying attention to them and gets what they are going through they are more okay with listening to advice and more willing to try things. Teachers make sure to create a space where everyones thoughts and ideas are welcome and respected. This makes students feel like school is not, about getting good grades but about becoming a good person who thinks carefully about things and does the right thing.

In a world where algorithms increasingly influence decision-making, the teacher remains a steady moral presence. As value mentors, educators ensure that technological advancement is accompanied by ethical awareness. They remind learners that while machines can process information, it is humans who must decide how that information is used.

School Culture and Leadership

A school that really cares about values can only happen when the school culture actually follows the principles it teaches. The culture of a school is not about the rules but also about how people talk to each other every day how decisions are made and what everyone expects from each other. When the people, in charge and the staff show respect and care about each other and take responsibility the students will learn these values too.

Leadership is really important when it comes to setting the tone. The leaders who show they are honest and fair make people feel safe. They make sure that teachers and students feel comfortable. What the leaders do shows that being a person and doing the right thing is what matters most. When we use AI in schools the leaders have to make sure that the technology we use is in line, with what the school believes in. The schools values should be the important thing, not the technology. Leadership has to make sure that technology does not take over the schools values. Leadership and the schools values go hand in hand with the use of AI.

Strong school culture encourages open dialogue, inclusivity, and collective responsibility. It creates space for diverse perspectives while maintaining shared moral anchors. When leadership intentionally nurtures such a culture, schools become communities that balance innovation with character, progress with purpose, and AI with compassion.

Community Engagement and Social Responsibility

Schools are not alone. They are a part of the community and the community is a part of them. The values that Schools teach affect the community and the community affects the values that Schools teach. When you think about it Schools and the community are connected in a way. Now that we have much technology around us it is even more important for Schools to be involved with the community. Technology is changing how we learn things how we make choices and how we get opportunities. So Schools need to stay connected, to the people they are helping and the community that schools are a part of.

Meaningful engagement starts when people talk to each other. When you have parents, local groups and community leaders talking about what students learn, technology and how students are doing people start to trust each other. It is good to be open about how we use AI tools like how we handle information how we grade students and how online platforms help students learn. This helps everyone understand what is going on. When people from the community have a say, new ideas are more likely to meet the needs of the community than just following what is popular. Meaningful engagement and community voices are important because they help make sure that innovation is useful to the community. Community leaders and parents and local organizations should be part of the conversation, about education and technology and student well-being.

Social responsibility goes beyond just talking about it. Schools can create learning experiences that actually connect students to the problems that people face every day in their own communities. When students work on projects that deal with things like taking care of the earth being smart about technology staying healthy or getting involved in their community they get to use what they learn to make a difference. Tools that use AI can be really helpful for doing research working together and coming up with solutions but the main goal is always to make a positive impact. Students start to understand that education is not about getting ahead personally but it is also, about contributing to the world and making it a better place.

Engagement is really good for equity. When we work with the community we can get more people to use spaces that are shared and we can get more people to be mentors and share what they know about the local area. Places like libraries and civic groups and companies can help make sure that technology is available to everyone and that people know about all the kinds of jobs they can have. When schools work closely with the people and places, around them it gives people a chance to succeed.

Community engagement is really important. It helps make sure that schools are accountable for what they do. When schools are open about what they're doing and ask for feedback they are more likely to listen to people and make good decisions. This is especially important when technology is changing fast. Community engagement helps schools make decisions that actually make sense for the people they are serving. This way schools do not get out of touch with what's really going on. Community engagement keeps schools connected to the community.

By anchoring education in social responsibility, schools ensure that technological progress is aligned with collective well-being. Students grow not only as capable individuals, but as informed and engaged members of society—prepared to use AI thoughtfully in service of the communities to which they belong.

Integrating AI Ethically

Integrating Artificial AI into schools is not about the technology. It is about what we think is right and wrong. The tools we pick the information we gather and the way we use these systems all show what our school really stands for. When we do this in an honest way we can make sure that new ideas help students learn without hurting their self respect being unfair or damaging the trust between teachers and students. Artificial AI should be used in a way that's good, for everyone.

The first thing that is important for integration is being clear, about what we want to do. We should use Artificial AI to make teaching to help more students and to support the growth of students. Not just because it is a new thing or because it can save time. When schools start by thinking about what they want to achieve with education technology starts to work with people to help them grow than controlling what they do.

Transparency is really important. Students and parents and educators need to know how these Artificial AI tools work. They should know what kind of data they are using and how they make decisions. When we explain things clearly people trust us more. They do not think that something strange is going on. Artificial AI should be easy to understand. We should be able to talk about it. It should not be something that's secret or that we cannot question. Transparency and openness are key, to using Artificial AI in a way.

Student data is very important. Artificial AI systems need to know a lot about students to make learning and to get useful information. Schools have to make sure they keep student information safe and private. This means they have to get permission from students and make sure nobody can access the information without authorization. Keeping student information safe is something schools have to do by law. It is also the right thing to do because students have the right to privacy and schools have to respect that. Student data and artificial AI systems go hand in hand so schools have to be careful, with student data.

Human oversight is really important. Artificial AI can look at patterns. Suggest things to do but the final decision should always be made by educators and leaders who understand the situation and all the little details. When we use technology in a way it helps educators make better decisions but it does not make the decisions for them. This way educators are still responsible for what happens. It reminds us that education is, about people working together.

So we need to keep checking if what we are doing is fair. When we get tools schools have to see how they affect people being treated equally and feeling good. We should ask teachers, students and families what they think. This helps us find out if something is not working right and make it better. Making sure we use these tools in a way is something we have to keep doing it is not something we just do once. Ethical practice and ethical integration of these tools is very important for our schools and for the people in them, like students and teachers and families. We have to keep working on ethical practice and ethical integration all the time.

When AI is integrated thoughtfully and responsibly, it becomes a supportive partner in learning. Anchored in purpose, transparency, and human oversight, ethical AI strengthens education while preserving the humanity at its core.

Leadership Strategies for Value Driven Ecosystems

The leaders of the school make sure that education is about values, like honesty and respect and that these values are part of the schools vision, rules and daily activities.

Leaders have to show the values they talk about. They need to use Artificial AI in a way communicate with respect be open to what others say and be fair when they make decisions. This shows that they are honest, in what they do. The way people behave is what really makes up the culture not just what they say. When leaders live by the values of the Artificial AI ecosystem other people are more likely to believe in the Artificial AI ecosystem values.

People need to keep talking and thinking about the ecosystem. Leaders should make sure there are places where people can look at how new technologies, like AI fit with what the institution believes in. The institution needs to check in to see if what they want to do is actually what they are doing and make changes when they need to. This way the ecosystem will be strong. Leaders and people at the institution need to keep looking at how new technologies, like AI are working with the institutions moral commitments.

Effective leadership in a value driven ecosystem balances innovation with integrity. By maintaining clarity, modeling principles, fostering collaboration, and ensuring accountability, leaders create learning environments where technological advancement supports—rather than overshadows—the human foundations of education.

Reflection question for leaders

- How clearly are school's core values reflected in our policies, curriculum, and use of AI tools?
- In what ways does AI driven leadership model help in ethical, transparent and inclusive decision making?
- Are the technology choices strengthening human connection and well-being, or unintentionally weakening them?
- How do we ensure that innovation aligns with purpose rather than convenience or trend?
- Whose voices are missing in our conversations about culture, values, and AI integration?
- What evidence shows that our school culture truly reflects the principles we claim to uphold?

CHAPTER 11

LIFELONG LEARNING AND THE FUTURE OF SCHOOL LEADERSHIP – LEADING IN THE AI ERA

The Changing Landscape of Leadership

School leadership is changing a lot because of technology and peoples ideas about work are changing too. The person in charge of a school has to do more than just make sure things run smoothly and watch over the academics. They have to deal with problems make sense of information in a fair way and make sure that new ideas and technology are good for people and help them grow. School leadership is really important, in this era of technology and it needs people who can handle all these new challenges. School leadership has to balance a lot of things and make sure that schools are still helping people learn and grow in a way.

Artificial AI is changing the way we make decisions. People in charge can now use tools to predict what will happen see how things are going right now and automate some tasks that help figure out how students are doing and what kind of support they need. These tools are really good, at giving us information and helping us understand things better. We have to be careful when we use them. Leaders need to think about what the information's telling us and also what it might be missing. Like the situation how people are feeling and what is going on with each individual student. Artificial AI is a part of this and we have to make sure we are using it in a way that takes all of these things into account.

The pace of change is really moving fast. Leaders have to stay on top of things because policies and the way we teach are changing all the time. People in charge need to keep learning all their lives it is not something they can choose to do or not. Leaders need to keep up with technologies and think about what is right and wrong. They also need to understand the rules for using things so they can make good decisions for their schools or organizations. Lifelong learning is very important, for leaders they need to do it to be effective. Leaders must understand emerging technologies and digital governance to lead their institutions in a way.

Leadership is really about people now. We live in a world where we are always looking at screens and dealing with technology. Because of this people want leaders who're real who care about them and who can explain things in a simple way. Leaders have to make people trust them even when things are not certain. They have to talk about things like privacy and fairness with data.. They have to make sure people understand the big decisions they make about technology. Leadership is about building trust and being honest, with people especially when it comes to technology and data.

The changing landscape of leadership is therefore defined by balance—between innovation and caution, efficiency and empathy, data and judgment. Leading in the AI era means remaining grounded in purpose while navigating constant transformation. Those who succeed will be learners first, capable of guiding their schools through change without losing sight of their human core.

Lifelong Learning for Leaders

In the time of AI the credibility of school leaders depends on their willingness to keep learning new things. The technology and rules are changing fast so what school leaders knew yesterday is not good enough today. For school leaders learning things all their life is not just something that is nice to do. It is something they have to do. School leaders have to keep learning about technology, new rules and new ways of teaching because school leaders have to stay up to date to be good, at their job.

Leaders who are good at their job make sure they really understand things like AI and how to use data in a fair way. They also need to know about governance and new ways of teaching people. You do not have to be an expert in these things. You have to know enough to make good choices.

Leaders need to ask the questions about things, like artificial AI being unfair and peoples private information being kept safe. They have to think about what will happen in the run if they start using new tools.

If leaders keep learning they will be able to make decisions that will help them in the future with artificial AI, data ethics, digital governance and new educational models.

Lifelong learning is not about technology. It is also about understanding people and how they interact with each other. The things that students need and the things that employers expect are always changing. Leaders have to stay on top of what's happening with different generations, what is going on with mental health and how people think about being successful.

Leaders need to talk to people in their field read about what is new and think about what they are doing. This helps leaders stay up to date and do what people need them to do. Lifelong learning helps leaders like this. It helps them understand things, like social dynamics and workforce expectations. Lifelong learning is important for leaders to keep doing a job.

It is really important to be humble. When leaders say they are still learning it helps everyone in the institution want to grow. Teachers feel okay to try things students see that the leaders are willing to change and innovation is something that everyone is a part of, not just something that the leaders tell them to do. Leaders and humility go hand in hand. When leaders have humility it makes a big difference. Leaders being humble helps everyone and innovation becomes a part of the culture not something that the leaders want.

We should have learning pathways that are structured to help us learn and grow. These include programs and communities where we learn from our peers. We also have mentorship circles. We work with people from other sectors. All of these things help us stay committed to what we do. We take the time to reflect on what we're doing and we give each other feedback. We also regularly review how we are leading. This helps us make changes when we need to because things are changing really fast around us. Leadership practices are, like the leadership programs we have. We review these regularly.

Ultimately, lifelong learning sustains ethical and effective leadership. It allows leaders to guide technological integration with discernment, respond to uncertainty with confidence, and remain grounded in purpose while navigating transformation. In the AI era, the most influential leaders are not those who claim to have all the answers, but those who remain committed to continual growth.

Leadership Competencies in the AI Era

To be a leader in the AI era you need to have a lot of different skills. You have to know about technology and also be able to make decisions that are fair and considerate of people. School leaders can not just stick to the ways of doing things they have to be able to deal with all the changes that are happening because of data, automation and new technology.

First of all you need to know about Digital and Data Literacy. This means you have to understand how AI systems work what kind of data they use and how they come up with answers. You do not have to be an expert but you have to be able to look at the numbers and figures and understand what they mean. You have to be able to ask questions and figure out if there are any problems or biases.

Making Ethical Decisions is also very important. Now that AI is being used in things like admissions and student support we have to think about if it's fair and private. Leaders have to think about what's right and what is in line with what their school believes in not just what is new or efficient.

You also have to be able to think on your feet and adapt to things. Technology and rules are changing all the time so leaders have to be able to adjust. This means trying things seeing how they work and changing your plan if you need to. You have to be able to stay calm when things are uncertain.

Being able to communicate with people in a way that's clear and honest is crucial. Leaders have to be able to explain technological decisions to teachers, students and families. If you talk to people openly and honestly they will trust you more. Be less anxious about new technology and data.

Leaders also have to be able to work with others. In the AI era you need to have teams of people with expertise like teachers, IT specialists and community partners. Leaders have to make sure that everyone has a say in the decisions that are made.

Finally you have to be able to bounce from challenges and think about what you are doing. As new technology keeps coming out leaders have to make sure they are not getting too caught up in the excitement. They have to think about what's best, for their school and their own well-being. If you take the time to reflect on what you're doing you can make sure you are moving in the right direction.

Leading Teacher Development

In the time of Artificial AI the development of teachers becomes one of the jobs of school leaders. As technology changes the classroom the way we test students and the way we teach leaders have to make sure teachers feel sure of themselves know what they are doing and have the support they need of feeling like they are in over their head.

The first thing to do is help teachers feel good about using tools. Teachers need to learn how to use Artificial AI tools, what they can do, where they're helpful, and when to be careful. The training teachers get should not just be about how to use the tools but about understanding the bigger picture: knowing when the tools might be biased using data in a responsible way and making sure humans are still in charge when Artificial AI is used to make decisions.

It is also very important to update the way we teach. Artificial AI can do jobs and give us information but it cannot replace the personal touch of a teacher the ability to make decisions based on the situation or the guidance that teachers give students. Leaders have to help teachers get better at the things that only humans can do. Like leading discussions, helping students think critically, mentoring students, and helping them grow emotionally. So training programs should balance learning about technology with thinking about how we teach.

Letting teachers learn at their pace is a good way to keep them interested. Not all teachers are equally good with technology. If we offer types of workshops, have teachers mentor each other, have coaches, and create groups where teachers can learn from each other teachers can grow at their own speed. When training is tailored to each teacher it respects their professionalism. Helps them become better teachers in a way that will last.

School leaders also have to create a culture where it's okay to try new things. Teachers should feel safe to try out lessons that use Artificial AI think about how they went and change what they do without being afraid of being judged. Leaders who see innovation as a way to learn than just following rules encourage creativity and taking thoughtful risks.

Having time and the right support is also crucial. Giving teachers time to learn, access to help and recognizing their efforts shows that the school is committed to helping them. Without these things well-planned programs will struggle to succeed. Schools need to remain closely connected to the communities they serve - the very people they exist to support. School leaders have to prioritize teacher development to make the most of Artificial AI, in the classroom and to help teachers become better at their jobs.

Data-Driven and AI-Supported Leadership

The time of Artificial AI is changing the way school leaders get information. Now they can see things like attendance and performance in time. When school leaders use data to make decisions they can make choices because they have more information.

Artificial AI systems can help school leaders see problems before they get big. They can see if a student is not doing well or if they are not coming to school. Then they can help that student with a plan. This way school leaders do not have to guess what to do they can use facts to make decisions.

Schools can also work efficiently. Artificial AI can help with things like scheduling and planning. This means school leaders have time to think about how to make the school better. Artificial AI tools can do tasks so school leaders can focus on more important things.

School leaders need to be careful when using data. They need to think about what the numbers mean. Numbers cannot tell us everything, like why studentsre motivated or how teachers feel. School leaders need to use their experience and judgment when making decisions with Artificial AI.

When school leaders are open about how they use data, people trust them more. When everyone understands how data is used to make decisions, they feel better about it. School leaders should explain what they are measuring and why and how they keep student information private. This way everyone knows what is going on. School leaders are accountable, for their decisions.

Ethical and Value Driven Leadership

In the time of AI leaders of schools need to be guided by ethics and strong values. This is not something that can be ignored it is essential. As schools start using technologies and systems to manage data leaders have to make sure that every new idea aligns with the basic principles of being fair respecting peoples dignity, including everyone and being accountable. If we make progress without thinking about what's right and wrong we risk losing the trust of people and weakening the schools reputation.

Leaders who care about ethics start by being clear about what their school stands for. They have to define the values of their institution and use those values to guide their decision making. When they are thinking about using artificial AI tools, policies or partnerships they need to ask themselves not just "Will this make things more efficient?". Also "Will this support our promise to be fair and care about the well-being of our students?"

Being fair is very important when it comes to using technology. Artificial AI systems can accidentally support ideas if we are not careful. Leaders who care about values demand that the companies they work with are transparent they carefully look at the sources of their data. They set up systems to make sure that the technology does not discriminate against certain groups. They know that technology is not automatically fair it has to be checked.

Being accountable makes ethical leadership stronger. Leaders should set up systems where decisions can be reviewed and where people can give feedback. Having policies about how data is managed, getting consent from people and setting up good communication systems ensures that everyone understands how information is used and protected. Ethical leaders welcome scrutiny they do not try to avoid it.

Caring about people. Being able to understand their feelings are still very important skills, for leaders. In a world where algorithms are increasingly influential, leaders have to protect the human side of education. Policies should prioritize the dignity of students the autonomy of teachers and the trust of the community. Technology should support relationships not replace them.

Finally leaders who care about values need to be brave. There may be pressured to quickly follow trends or to prioritize results that can be measured over long-term impact. Ethical leaders are willing to slow down, ask questions and even say no to new ideas if they conflict with the principles of their institution.

In the time of AI leaders are tested not just by how well they manage change but by how responsibly they guide it. When values guide every decision schools can make progress with technology while still protecting the values that make education meaningful.

Framework: Leadership for Change in AI Education

Change in AI-integrated education system requires structured and a flexible framework that aligns innovation with institutional values. This change has to be purpose-driven, ethically grounded, and strategically planned.

1. Figure Out The Goal

Every time we start something new with Artificial AI we need to know why we are doing it. The people in charge have to make sure that using this technology is going to help us achieve our goals in education making learning available to more people, making sure everyone is included or making things run more smoothly. If we know what we want to achieve we will not just do something because it is trendy or because someone else is doing it.

2. Being Fair. Responsible

We need to have clear rules about how we use peoples personal information how we are transparent how we get permission and who is responsible for what. We should also have a group of people who check that the Artificial AI tools we use are okay with what our institution believes in. We have to decide who makes the decisions how we choose which tools to use and how we deal with problems that might come up.

3. Helping People Get Ready

If we want to make a change we have to make sure people are ready for it. The people in charge have to help teachers learn things, get better with technology and understand what is right and wrong. If we keep training, work together and help each other we will be able to use Artificial AI in a way that lasts.

4. Talking To Everyone Involved

We have to talk to teachers, students, families and our partners in the community so that they trust us. The people in charge should create ways for us to talk about things answer questions honestly and listen to what people have to say. If we include everyone they will feel like what we are doing is fair.

5. Try It Out Think About It Make It Better

Of trying to do everything at once we should try a little bit at a time. If we start small we can see what works and what does not. Then we can make changes. We have to keep checking to make sure that the Artificial AI tools are doing what they are supposed to do and not causing any problems.

6. Always Be Ready To Learn

Using Artificial AI is not something we do once. Then forget about. The people in charge have to help us get used to changing, thinking about what we're doing and being willing to try new things. We have to make it a part of who we're, as an institution so we can keep getting better.

Reflection Questions for Leaders

- Is our approach to AI integration clearly aligned with our educational purpose and core values?
- How confident are we that our data practices protect privacy, fairness, and transparency?

- Are we building sufficient capacity among teachers to use AI responsibly and effectively?
- Do our decisions reflect evidence from data while still honoring human context and professional judgment?
- How are we ensuring that innovation reduces inequity rather than widening existing gaps?
- What mechanisms are in place to review, refine, and recalibrate our AI strategies over time?

CHAPTER 12

GLOBAL AI ADAPTATION

Artificial AI is not being used all over the world. Some countries are creating classrooms that use Artificial AI and research centers while others are still trying to get an internet connection. The way Artificial AI is being used around the world is affected by things like roads and buildings laws, money and what politicians want to achieve.

The way countries are using Artificial AI is very different from one place to another. The United States, some parts of Europe and East Asia are using Artificial AI a lot. They started using it very quickly. Many parts of Africa, South Asia and Latin America are also using Artificial AI. They are doing it as part of a bigger plan to improve their technology and they have to deal with basic problems like getting everyone connected to the internet and training teachers.

Developed countries versus developing countries

Countries that are already developed usually start using Artificial AI faster because they have good technology and a lot of money for research. Countries like the United States, Japan and Germany have universities and research centers that help them use Artificial AI in schools and businesses.

Developing countries, like India, Brazil and Kenya are also using Artificial AI. It is not happening evenly. Schools in cities may start using Artificial AI but schools in rural areas may not have the technology they need. The difference is not about how much countries want to use Artificial AI. It is also about whether they are ready to use it.

The role of governments, businesses and universities

For countries to use Artificial AI well, governments, businesses and universities need to work.

Governments decide what to do about Artificial AI by creating plans and deciding how to spend money. For example China has made Artificial AI a top priority. Finland is teaching people about Artificial AI so they can use it.

Businesses create Artificial AI tools and make them available to schools sometimes faster than governments can make rules about them. Universities do research teach people about Artificial AI and help make sure it is used responsibly. When governments businesses and universities work together they can create a system for using Artificial AI.

Artificial AI is a geopolitical priority

Artificial AI is not a new technology. It is also a way for countries to compete with each other and have more influence in the world. Because of this schools are becoming more important in teaching people about Artificial AI and preparing the generation of innovators.

The global shift to Artificial AI is not about how fast countries can adopt it. It is also about how they can use it in a responsible and fair way. The real challenge for education is not just to keep up with technology but to shape it in a way that is good, for everyone.

National AI Strategies in Education

As Artificial AI becomes central to economic growth and national competitiveness, many countries have moved beyond pilot projects and drafted formal AI strategies that include education reform as a core pillar. These roadmaps typically focus on curriculum redesign, teacher preparedness, research investment, and partnerships with industry.

Some countries have put Artificial AI into their plans for education.

China has taken an approach that is driven by the government. Artificial AI is a priority, supported by government money, research centers and inclusion in schools and universities. The goal is term: building expertise in China while teaching people about Artificial AI from an early age.

The United States does things a bit differently. The government gives some guidance. It is mostly up to the states, universities and private technology companies to make things happen. How much Artificial AI is used varies from place to place. The country has a lot of new companies and research universities that help try out new Artificial AI tools for learning.

Finland is focused on teaching people about Artificial AI from an age not just experts. Of just focusing on advanced research the plan is to help people understand Artificial AI concepts so everyone knows about it not just people who work with it.

India has a mix of approaches. With digital projects and national plans to teach people new skills Artificial AI education is closely tied to helping people get jobs. The government has goals trying to reach all kinds of people in cities and rural areas.

Curriculum Reforms: Embedding AI Literacy

A common thread across national strategies is curriculum reform. AI literacy is gradually being integrated at multiple levels:

- Foundational digital literacy in primary education
- Computational thinking and coding in middle school
- Data science, machine learning, and ethics in secondary and higher education

Importantly, AI education is not limited to engineering streams. Many systems are incorporating ethics, societal impact, and critical thinking into AI-related modules to prepare students for responsible use.

Teacher Training and Digital Upskilling

No national AI strategy succeeds without teachers. Governments increasingly recognize that educator readiness determines implementation quality.

Teacher training programs now focus on:

- Basic AI awareness
- Practical classroom applications
- Data literacy
- Ethical use of AI tools

In many countries, digital upskilling initiatives target both new teachers and experienced educators, ensuring AI integration does not widen generational gaps within the profession.

AI in classrooms across continent

AI is not something you find in research labs or policy documents anymore. It is actually inside classrooms now. It is changing how students learn, how teachers grade and how schools work.. What AI looks like can be very different depending on where you are what resources you have and what kind of infrastructure is in place.

Adaptive Learning Platforms

These adaptive learning systems use data to change what students learn in time. Of every student getting the same lesson they get exercises that are just right for them based on how they are doing. In some parts of North America, Europe and East Asia these systems are already part of schooling and they help students learn in a way that is just for them.

In places where resources are limited these adaptive platforms are often only used in small test programs or in private schools in cities. When the infrastructure is good it is possible to give every student an education. When the infrastructure is not good personalized education is something people hope for.

AI Tutors and Learning Assistants

AI-powered tutors and chat-based helpers are assisting students with their homework getting ready for exams and understanding concepts. These tools give students feedback away and are available all the time, which is especially helpful in big classrooms where teachers cannot give every student individual attention.

In schools that have a lot of resources AI tutors help teachers do their jobs. In schools that do not have a lot of resources AI tutors sometimes have to fill in for teachers. How well AI tutors work depends on how teachers use them: when teachers use them as a tool to help make learning better; when teachers use them as a replacement they can make students think less critically.

Automated Assessments

AI is also changing how students are evaluated. Automated grading systems can grade tests away and can even look at written work to see how well it is organized how well it makes sense and how original it is. This means teachers have work to do and can give students feedback faster.

People are still worried about automated grading systems being biased not understanding the context and relying too much on algorithms to grade. Countries where the government watches over education closely and where teachers are trained well tend to use automated assessments carefully.

Language Translation for Multilingual Education

In places where many languages are spoken AI-driven translation tools are helping students learn. Tools that can translate languages in time and turn speech into text are bridging the gap between languages especially in countries, with many different languages.

For students who are learning in a language that's not their first language these tools can make a big difference.. How well they work depends on how good the data is and how well the tools understand different languages. Languages that do not have a lot of digital data often do not get translated as well.

Workforce alignment and economic impact

As Artificial AI changes industries people are looking at education systems to see how they can be changed to fit the kinds of jobs that are coming. The big question for countries is not if Artificial AI will change the job market. How fast education can keep up?

Governments are starting to connect their plans for Artificial AI with plans for the workforce. They are changing what schools teach what universities offer and what people can learn in training to match the demand for things like data science, automation, robotics, cybersecurity and Artificial AI ethics.

In some countries like Singapore and Germany the government plans the workforce closely with what industries need so there is a clear path from technical school to a job. In countries like India and the United States new companies and startups are driving the demand, for people who know about Artificial AI, so universities and certification programs are changing to meet this demand.

The focus is changing from getting a degree to getting the skills that are needed to do a job. Artificial AI is a part of this change and education systems need to teach people the skills they need to work with Artificial AI.

Automation, Job Creation, and Reskilling at Scale

Automation raises legitimate concerns about job displacement, particularly in routine and repetitive roles. However, history shows that technological shifts also generate new categories of employment.

AI is creating demand for:

- Data analysts
- AI trainers and auditors
- Human-machine interaction specialists
- Ethics and compliance professionals

The challenge lies in timing. Job displacement can occur faster than job creation if reskilling systems are slow or inaccessible.

Nations that invest in scalable reskilling—supported by public funding, digital infrastructure, and industry partnerships—are better positioned to manage workforce transitions smoothly.

International collaboration

The Artificial AI adaptation process does not take place on its own. Even though national strategies determine the direction the development and governance of Artificial AI are closely connected. Things like research networks and shared datasets and global supply chains and talent flows from one country to another make Artificial AI a business.

Cross-Border Research Partnerships

Universities and technology companies and governments often work together across borders on Artificial AI research. They set up labs and exchange students and create innovation hubs with many countries involved to speed up breakthroughs in machine learning and robotics and Artificial AI in healthcare and climate modeling.

Institutions in countries like the United States and the United Kingdom and Japan often write research papers together. Share ways to fund their research. Countries that are still growing their economies are joining these networks. Contributing data from their regions and ideas from their research and different environments to test things.

These collaborations mean that people do not have to do the work twice and they help raise the standards of research around the world. At the time they need agreements on who owns the ideas and how to govern the data and keep it secure.

Global Artificial AI Ethics Frameworks

As Artificial AI systems affect education and jobs and healthcare and governance it becomes very important to have some coordination on ethics. Questions about bias and transparency and accountability and student data privacy cannot be answered within one countrys borders.

Organizations like UNESCO and the OECD have come up with principles for Artificial AI that focus on rights and inclusivity and responsible innovation. These frameworks guide the policies of countries while encouraging them to work across regions.

It is especially important to have shared principles in education, where Artificial AI tools shape what students learn and how they are assessed. Shared principles help prevent standards in different places that could put some students at a disadvantage.

Knowledge Sharing Between Nations

Apart from agreements countries can learn from each other by sharing policies and doing pilot studies and documenting their experiences. Countries that have already integrated Artificial AI into their systems can offer lessons on how to do it and countries that are just starting out can contribute ideas for low-cost or scalable models.

Sharing knowledge reduces the risk. Makes the policy process faster. It also helps countries adapt to situations—what works in one place can be improved and applied in another place with sensitivity to the local culture.

Multilateral Initiatives

Multilateral forums are now including Artificial AI governance in their discussions. Groups, like the G20 are talking about the impact of Artificial AI and how it affects the workforce and digital inclusion. Regional alliances are working together to coordinate standards and make it easier for systems to work together and for trade to happen.

These initiatives recognize that Artificial AI systems operate across borders—through cloud platforms and global companies and shared data infrastructures. Working together helps balance innovation with stability. Makes sure that Artificial AI benefits everyone.

Global Case Study: National Pathways for AI in Education

The integration of AI into schools is no longer a theoretical debate but a strategic reality. However, nations are bifurcated between proactive systemic integration and cautious, risk-based frameworks.

1. Estonia: The Proactive "AI Leap"

Estonia is the global benchmark for systemic AI adoption, treating technology as a tool for national digital sovereignty.

- **Strategy:** Launched in September 2025, the "AI Leap" initiative aims to provide every student and teacher with high-quality AI tools.
- **Key Action:** Rather than banning AI, the government provided access to ChatGPT Edu to 20,000 high school students in its first phase.
- **Teacher Focus:** The program emphasizes "mass training" to ensure educators know more about AI's capabilities and threats than their students.

2. Ireland: The Cautious and Deliberative Stance

Ireland represents a measured approach that prioritizes academic integrity and risk mitigation over rapid speed.

- **Strategy:** The Irish Department of Education released guidance in late 2025 that delegates final decision-making power to individual school boards.
- **Key Challenge:** Teacher unions (ASTI) have resisted reforms that increase the weight of project-based work, fearing that AI makes cheating in the Leaving Certificate nearly impossible to detect.

3. Singapore: The Systematic "Smart Nation" Model

Singapore employs a centralized, highly structured approach focused on AI literacy as a core 21st-century competency.

- **Strategy:** The AI for Students (AI4S) program integrates AI concepts across multiple subjects, not just computer science.
- **Key Innovation:** AI-enabled companions provide students with customized feedback and motivation, while machine learning systems help teachers identify when students are struggling in real time.

4. China: The Large-Scale Innovation Hub

China leads in large-scale deployment, leveraging private-sector partnerships and massive data sets to optimize test performance.

- **Strategy:** AI is a "national priority," with significant investments in intelligent tutoring systems like Squirrel AI that adapt content to millions of students simultaneously.
- **Trade-offs:** While highly efficient, the Chinese model has faced criticism for prioritizing exam results over data privacy and student surveillance.

5. United States: The Fragmented Innovation Landscape

The U.S. approach is defined by a lack of a single national mandate, leading to a fragmented landscape of innovation driven by state policies and private tech giants.

- **Strategy:** The federal government provides ethical frameworks (e.g., "Artificial AI and the Future of Teaching and Learning"), but actual implementation is decided by states and local districts.
- **Key Player:** The private sector (e.g., Khan Academy) acts as a primary laboratory for new AI features, while universities use AI chatbots like Georgia State's "Pounce" to reduce student "summer melt".

Conclusion

The future of AI in education depends on moving from reactive bans to proactive literacy. While leaders like Estonia and Singapore demonstrate the power of systemic support, the global "AI Divide" remains a significant risk. Success requires balancing technological innovation with the human-centered values of empathy, critical thinking, and social-emotional development.

The Future

As AI continues to reshape societies, education systems must move beyond reactive adoption and toward intentional design. The future will not be defined by which country deploys the most technology, but by which systems balance scale, ethics, and human development effectively.

A Shared AI Literacy Baseline

We need to start with the basics when it comes to Artificial AI. Every person should have an understanding of Artificial AI just like we all need to know how to read and use computers. This means knowing about algorithms, data, automation and the ethical implications of Artificial AI.

Artificial AI is a part of our daily lives it affects our jobs and the decisions we make. So every student, no matter where they live should have an understanding of Artificial AI. If we do this it will help reduce inequality and people will be able to think about Artificial AI systems.

A shared Artificial AI literacy baseline is important. It means every student will have the basic knowledge of Artificial AI, which will help them in the long run.

Ethical-First Design Principles

When we think about the future of education we need to put ethics. This means thinking about transparency, fairness, accountability and data privacy when we design technologies for the classroom. We should not just think about these things after we have already created the technology.

There are organizations like UNESCO and the OECD that provide guidance on how to make sure Artificial AI is used in a way that respects rights and includes everyone. If we follow these principles we can make sure that innovation does not hurt students or make things unfair.

If we put ethics first it will also help build trust between teachers, parents and students. This is very important if we want to make sure that new technologies are used in a way that's good for everyone.

Blended Human-AI Pedagogy

The classroom of the future will not be completely run by machines. It will not reject technology either. It will be a mix of both.

Artificial AI can help personalize the things we learn analyze how we learn and give us feedback away. Teachers are still very important because they can provide guidance help us understand things in context and teach us about emotions and ethics. This way of teaching, which combines humans and Artificial AI makes the teachers job stronger not weaker.

We still need human judgment to understand things to be creative and to think critically. These are skills that Artificial AI systems cannot fully replace.

Scalable Yet Culturally Sensitive Systems

If we want to create an education system that works everywhere we need to make sure it can be used by people without losing the unique culture of each place. Artificial AI tools should be able to be adapted to languages, histories and ways of teaching.

If we can make the system work for people it will be more efficient and will reach more people.. We also need to make sure it respects the culture of each place so it is relevant and includes everyone. If we balance these two things we can prevent technology from making everything the same.

Artificial AI should be used in a way that helps everyone no matter where they live or what their culture is. We need to make sure that Artificial AI systems are scalable and culturally sensitive, at the time. This is the way we can create an education system that really works for everyone.

CHAPTER 13

REIMAGINING EDUCATION – A LEADERSHIP CALL TO ACTION

Reimagining education in the AI era is a task that needs more than just new tools in the classroom. It needs a plan that brings together technology, human values, leadership, teaching methods and community into one direction. This plan means connecting ideas like ethics, inclusion, lifelong learning, teacher development and data-informed leadership into one shared goal for education.

At the heart of this plan is an idea: technology is a tool, not the main goal. Artificial AI can help make learning personal make things easier to manage and give people access to knowledge. The real goal of education is still to help people become thoughtful, capable and responsible individuals. When schools use AI in a way that focuses on growth they make sure that new ideas do not overshadow what is important.

This plan also makes sure that fairness is a principle. Access to tools, good teaching and data-driven insights should not make it harder for some people to catch up. Instead AI should be used to find gaps in learning provide help where it is needed and give opportunities to people who do not have as much. Inclusion becomes a part of the plan not something

Leaders play a role in making this plan work. Clear communication, ethical decision-making and consistently showing values help everyone work together. When leaders explain how each new idea fits into the plan it helps prevent confusion and makes things clearer. Teachers, students and families can then see how new ideas help move things forward.

Another important thing is to balance what is happening in the world with what's happening in our own community. While AI tools are used over the world, they need to be used in a way that makes sense for our community, our culture and our schools. A good plan uses technology to meet local needs rather than just following what others are doing.

Finally making this plan work requires thought and reflection. As AI gets better schools need to keep checking if they are still doing things that fit their goals. Getting feedback reviewing ethics and talking to each other help keep things clear when things are changing.

Reimagining education is not about getting rid of what we have but about making it better, on purpose. When technology, values, leadership and learning are all connected schools can move forward with confidence. Using ideas while still keeping the human part of education that matters.

A Call to Action

Reimagining education in the AI era is really important. It is something that we need to do now. The decisions we make today about using technology what our leaders think is important making sure everyone is treated fairly and being careful about what's right and wrong will affect how students learn, think and contribute to society in the future.

This is a time when leaders need to take charge. Schools cannot just see what happens with AI. They need to take control of how AI's used in their schools. We should use ideas to help students, not just because we feel like we have to. Every time we make a decision we need to ask ourselves: does this help all students learn feel good about themselves and have opportunities?

Teachers need to keep learning. They need to be curious, think about what they're doing and be open to new ideas. Leaders need to create a place where teachers can try new things talk to each other and remember what is important. Communities need to get involved ask questions and work together so that education is what we all want it to be.

The future of education will not just be about computers and digital tools. It will be about how schools use technology to help people. We all need to work but leaders need to make some tough decisions.

Now is the time to take action in a ethical and brave way. We must ensure that as AI reshapes the world, education plays a guiding role in steering those changes. In the age of AI, education must evolve with intention and purpose. We need to think about how AI's used in education and make sure it is used to help students and society.

www.ingramcontent.com/pod-product-compliance
Lightning Source LLC
Chambersburg PA
CBHW020240250926
51848CB00007BA/513
* 9 7 8 9 3 6 0 7 0 9 4 6 4 *